EXCEL 2024

YOUR NO-FUSS GUIDE
TO MASTERING FUNCTIONS,
FORMULAS, AND CHARTS

FROM BEGINNER TO ADVANCED IN 7 DAYS

DEREK COLLINS

Copyright © 2023 by Chapter Zero LLC

All rights reserved. No portion of this book may be reproduced in any form without written permission from the publisher or author, except as permitted by U.S. copyright law.

This publication is designed to provide accurate and authoritative information in regard to the subject matter covered. While the publisher and author have used their best efforts in preparing this book, they make no representations or warranties with respect to the accuracy or completeness of the contents of this book and specifically disclaim any implied warranties of merchantability or fitness for a particular purpose. Neither the publisher nor the author shall be liable for any loss of profit or any other commercial damages, including but not limited to special, incidental, consequential, personal, or other damages.

The mention of Excel and Microsoft in this book is for informational purposes only and is not intended to infringe upon any trademark or intellectual property rights held by Microsoft Corporation. Excel and Microsoft are registered trademarks of Microsoft Corporation and are used here only to refer to the software and company, respectively. No endorsement or affiliation with Microsoft Corporation is implied or intended.

Published by Chapter Zero (www.chapterzerobooks.com)
Email: info@chapterzerobooks.com
Edited by Melissa Fields
Book Cover by Karen Davies

First Edition – November 2023
Paperback ISBN: 978-1-961963-13-9
Hardback ISBN: 978-1-961963-14-6

Contents

INTRODUCTION   1

1. DAY 1: INTRODUCING EXCEL   3
   An Introduction To The Interface
   The Ribbon
   The Quick Access Toolbar
   The Formula Bar
   The Status Bar
   Mastering Basic Operations
   Data Entry Essentials
   Enhancing Data Entry
   Basic Formatting Techniques
   Basic Math Operations

2. DAY 2: FORMULAS AND FUNCTIONS   23
   Understanding Excel Formulas: Syntax and Usage
   Relative and Absolute Cell References
   Common Excel Functions: SUM, AVERAGE, COUNT, MIN, MAX
   Introduction to Logical Functions: IF, AND, OR
   Advanced Functions
   Error Handling in Formulas

3. DAY 3: DATA MANAGEMENT   43
   Sorting and Filtering Data
   Combining Sorting and Filtering
   Introduction to Conditional Formatting
   Handling Large Datasets: Removing duplicates, Data Validation
   Basic Text Functions: LEFT, RIGHT, MID, CONCATENATE, TEXT
   Date and Time Functions

4. DAY 4: DATA VISUALIZATION   61
   Creating Charts and Graphs
   Choosing the Right Chart Type for Your Data

    Customizing and Formatting Your Charts
    Introduction to Sparklines
    Visualizing Different Types of Data
    Data Visualization Best Practices

5. DAY 5: INTERMEDIATE FUNCTIONS AND FEATURES   81
    Introduction to Lookup Functions: VLOOKUP, HLOOKUP, INDEX/MATCH
    Understanding Pivot Tables: Creation and customization
    Advanced Conditional Formatting Techniques
    Array Formulas and Functions
    Dynamic Arrays and Spill Range
    Array Formulas with Conditional Logic
    Best Practices and Practical Applications
    Linking, Embedding, and Importing Data

6. DAY 6: ADVANCED EXCEL FEATURES   101
    Collaborative Editing and Co-Authoring
    Introduction to Macros and VBA
    Basic Automation
    Introduction to Excel Power Query and Power Pivot
    Handling Multidimensional Data
    Advanced Charting Techniques

7. DAY 7: MASTERING EXCEL   119
    Optimizing Workflow
    Keyboard and Mouse Tricks
    Customizing the Quick Access Toolbar
    Integration with Other Office Applications
    Excel Security
    Staying Ahead with Excel
    Excel for Mobile Devices
    Excel Troubleshooting

CONCLUSION   139

Acknowledgements   141

INTRODUCTION

In today's digital world, knowing how to navigate Excel has gone from a valuable asset to an absolute necessity. Excel is not just a software application—it's a game-changer, a time-saver, and, for many, the backbone of their daily professional lives. Whether you're an entrepreneur looking to optimize your business, a student crunching data for a research project, or an aspiring analyst in the bustling corporate world, Excel is a tool that can turn the tedious into the manageable and the complicated into the comprehensible.

But let's be honest—Excel can feel like a beast. The labyrinth of functions and formulas can be intimidating, even for those with a knack for numbers. Have you ever found yourself staring at an error message, feeling utterly lost? Or struggled to translate a sea of data into a simple, insightful chart? And how about those elusive pivot tables and lookup functions? We've all been there. And that's why you've picked up this book.

And with the release of Excel 2024, the game has changed even more dramatically. This latest version introduces groundbreaking features that redefine what we can achieve with this already powerful tool. Dynamic data types bring unprecedented efficiency and connectivity to your data, linking it seamlessly to the world and ensuring it stays updated. The integration with Microsoft Teams ushers in a new era of collaboration, making Excel a central hub for team-based data management and decision-making. The introduction of Natural Language Processing means that interacting with Excel is more intuitive than ever, allowing you to use simple, conversational queries to analyze and visualize data. And with AI-powered insights, Excel now assists in data analysis and proactively guides you toward meaningful insights through intelligent pattern recognition and visualization suggestions. These advancements, along with enhanced data visualization capabilities, smarter data import and transformation tools, and significant enhancements to Excel for the web, make Excel 2024 an essential tool for anyone dealing with data in any capacity.

This guide is your ticket to mastering Excel, regardless of your current skill level. No more feeling overwhelmed by the vast array of options or frustrated by recurring errors. I've structured this guide into seven manageable chapters, each designed to build your skills progressively. While Ie've organized the content to offer a 7-day crash course, you're free to set your own pace and take as much time as you need on each chapter.

Each day is a step forward, gradually building your knowledge from the ground up. And the best part is that I've designed this course in a way that encourages learning by doing—because I know that Excel is best understood when it's applied.

Day one will help you find your footing, introducing you to the Excel interface and guiding you through basic operations. As the days progress, we'll venture into formulas, functions, data management, and visualization, ensuring you have a solid grasp of these critical areas. We'll then transition into intermediate and advanced features, such as pivot tables, VBA, and automation. As the week wraps up, you'll find yourself effortlessly mastering Excel, ready to tackle even the trickiest tasks with confidence.

Let me tell you something; this is not just a book—it's an investment in your personal and professional development. With every page turned, you're arming yourself with the skills to increase your productivity, make better data-driven decisions, and potentially open new doors in your career.

Are you eager to put those Excel frustrations behind you? Ready to unlock the full potential of this amazing software? If you're nodding along, buckle up for an exciting, empowering journey. Let's turn you into an Excel pro in just 7 days!

Let's hit the road!

Chapter One

DAY 1: INTRODUCING EXCEL

At its core, Excel is a spreadsheet program, a digital evolution of the paper ledger sheets that have been used in accounting and data analysis for centuries. Spreadsheets allow you to arrange data in rows and columns, providing a straightforward way to store, manage, and manipulate information.

Microsoft Excel was first released in 1985 and has since undergone numerous updates and revisions. It has evolved from a simple spreadsheet program to a powerful tool equipped with a multitude of functions, from basic arithmetic calculations to complex data analysis and visualization techniques. Excel's versatility makes it indispensable in a variety of fields, including finance, healthcare, engineering, and beyond.

On Day 1, you'll get acquainted with the essentials that form the backbone of any Excel project. From understanding the interface and mastering basic operations to getting comfortable with data entry and formatting techniques, you'll touch upon the fundamental aspects that make Excel a powerful tool for a wide range of tasks. These basics are more than just starting points – they're the essential skills that will give you the confidence to take on increasingly complex challenges as you move forward.

An Introduction To The Interface

Our first stop is familiarizing ourselves with the terrain—Excel's user interface. This is where all your work in Excel will take place, and becoming comfortable here is the first step towards becoming an Excel pro. Let's go over the key elements of this digital landscape.

The Ribbon - Think of the Ribbon as Excel's command center. The wide, horizontal strip at the top of your Excel workspace holds most of the commands you'll use. It's divided into tabs (like Home, Insert, and Formulas), and each of these tabs houses a specific collection of tools and options. I'll show you how to find your way around the Ribbon, discover hidden tools, and customize it to your preferences.

The Quick Access Toolbar - This is your personal toolbox in Excel. It's a small, customizable toolbar at the top of the Excel window. It provides quick access to commands you use frequently. We'll learn how to add or remove tools from this toolbar to streamline your workflow.

The Formula Bar - Think of the Formula Bar as your spotlight in Excel. Located just below the Ribbon, it's where you'll see and edit the data or formula in the currently selected cell. Later on, you will find out how to use it to enter and edit data, create formulas, and more.

The Status Bar - The Status Bar is like your dashboard in Excel. A thin strip at the bottom of your Excel window provides brief information about the selected cells and offers quick, one-click access to some handy Excel features. Examining every icon on the Status Bar, we'll discover their purposes and see how you can adjust them to present the information that suits your needs.

As we progress, we'll get into the nitty-gritty of these elements, helping you get a handle on what they're all about and showing you how you can fine-tune them to match your personal preferences.

The Ribbon

The Ribbon is basically the control panel of Excel, a wide horizontal strip at the top of your workspace. It's where you'll find almost all the commands, tools, and features you'll need to perform tasks ranging from the basics, like data entry, to more advanced functions, such as running complex formulas.

The Ribbon is organized into a series of tabs, each dedicated to a specific set of tasks. Clicking on a tab reveals a fresh array of tools and options customized to the specific functions associated with that tab. For example, clicking on the 'Home' tab will show tools related to basic formatting and data manipulation, while the 'Insert' tab will offer options for adding various elements like charts and images to your worksheet.

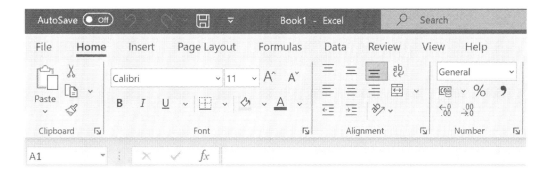

The 'Home' Tab

You'll find yourself frequently working on the 'Home' tab in Excel, especially in the beginning. This tab is the go-to place for basic commands. Here, you'll find a variety of tools neatly grouped into sections.

For instance, in the 'Font' section, you can change the font type, size, and color. The 'Alignment' section allows you to adjust how your text sits within cells—whether centered, aligned to the left or right, or even angled. The 'Number' section lets you format how numbers, dates, and times are displayed. Additionally, you'll find indispensable data editing tools like 'Sort & Filter,' which allows you to organize your data, and 'Find & Select,' which helps you locate specific pieces of information within your worksheet.

The 'Insert' Tab

Moving on to the 'Insert' tab, this is your creative playground in Excel. Want to add a chart to visualize your data? You'll find it here. Need to insert a picture or a shape? This is the place. The 'Insert' tab is also where you can add pivot tables, an advanced feature that allows you to summarize and analyze large sets of data in a more manageable format.

The 'Page Layout' Tab

The 'Page Layout' tab is where you'll manage how your Excel worksheet appears both on-screen and in printed form. Here, you can set your margins, adjust the orientation between portrait and landscape, and manage the size of your worksheet.

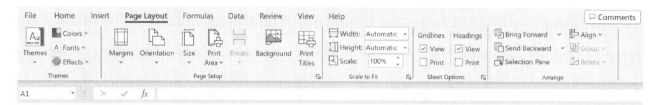

You'll also find options for setting the print area and inserting page breaks, which are crucial when you're preparing documents for printing. Additionally, this tab allows you to control gridlines and headings, offering you the flexibility to decide whether or not they appear on the printed page.

The 'Formulas' Tab

This tab is your mathematical hub in Excel. Here, you'll find various formulas categorized into different types, such as 'Financial,' 'Logical,' 'Text,' 'Date and Time,' and many more. Each category opens up a dropdown menu with a list of specific formulas you can use.

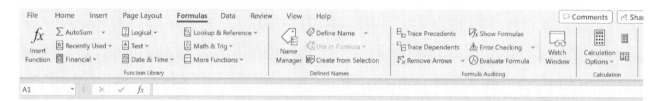

For example, under 'Financial,' you'll find formulas like PMT for calculating loan payments and FV for future value of investments. The 'Formulas' tab is also where you can access the 'Function Library,' which provides a more detailed explanation and examples of how each formula works.

The 'Data' Tab

When it comes to anything related to data manipulation and analysis in Excel, the 'Data' tab is where you want to be. This tab offers powerful tools like 'Sort' and 'Filter,' which allow you to organize your data in various ways. You'll also find the 'Data Validation' feature, which lets you set rules for what kind of data can be entered into a cell.

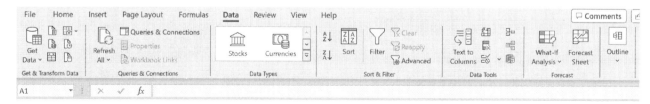

Another key feature is 'Text to Columns,' which can separate text within a cell into multiple cells based on a delimiter, such as a comma or space. For those dealing with external data, the 'Get

& Transform Data' section provides options to import data from various sources like databases, online services, and even other Excel workbooks.

The 'Review' Tab

This tab is essential for collaborative work and document finalization. Here, you'll find the 'Spelling' checker and 'Thesaurus,' which help ensure the quality of text within your worksheet. The 'Comments' section allows you to insert notes and feedback without altering the actual content.

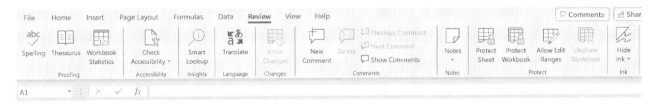

This tab also offers 'Track Changes' and 'Protect Sheet/Workbook,' which can be a real lifesaver when multiple people are working on the same document. They help you keep an eye on edits and prevent unauthorized changes.

The 'View' Tab

The 'View' tab controls how your Excel workspace appears on your screen. You can switch between different worksheet views like 'Normal,' 'Page Layout,' and 'Page Break Preview.' This tab also offers the 'Zoom' feature, allowing you to zoom in or out of your worksheet for better visibility. If you're working with multiple worksheets or workbooks, the 'Window' section provides options like 'New Window' and 'Arrange All,' which help you manage these multiple windows effectively.

The 'Help' Tab

Lastly, the 'Help' tab is your built-in guide within Excel. If you're stuck or need to learn how to do something, this is the place to go. You can type in your query, and Excel will provide you with a list of related help articles, video tutorials, and

step-by-step guides. It's an indispensable resource for both beginners and advanced users.

Customizing the Ribbon

Customizing the Ribbon to your needs and preferences can save you time and make your experience with Excel more efficient. Here's how you can go about it:

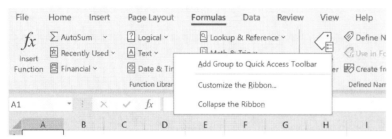

Accessing Ribbon Customization Options - To start customizing the Ribbon, you'll first need to access the customization options. You can do this by right-clicking on any empty space within the Ribbon and selecting "Customize the Ribbon." Alternatively, you can go to 'File' > 'Options' and then click on 'Customize Ribbon' in the Excel Options dialog box that appears.

Understanding the Customization Panel - Once you're in the customization panel, you'll see two main columns. The column on the right represents the current Ribbon tabs and their contents, while the column on the left lists all the commands you can add to the Ribbon. You can toggle between different sets of commands by selecting options from the dropdown menu at the top of the left column, such as 'Popular Commands,' 'Commands Not in the Ribbon,' or 'All Commands.'

Adding New Tabs and Groups - You can add a new tab by clicking the 'New Tab' button at the bottom of the right column. A new tab, labeled "New Tab (Custom)" will appear. You can rename it by right-clicking and selecting 'Rename.' Inside each tab, you'll see 'New Group (Custom),' which is a container for commands. You can also rename groups to better reflect the commands you'll place in them.

Adding Commands to Groups - To add a command to a group, first select the command from the left column. Then, select the group in the right column where you want to add the command and click the 'Add > >' button between the two columns. The command will now appear in the selected group on the Ribbon.

Reordering and Removing Items - You can change the order of tabs, groups, and commands by selecting them and using the 'Move Up' and 'Move Down' buttons at the bottom of the right column. To remove an item, select it and click 'Remove.'

Resetting the Ribbon - If you ever want to return to the default Ribbon settings, simply click the 'Reset' button at the bottom of the right column and choose 'Reset all customizations.'

Finalizing Your Customizations - Once you're satisfied with your customizations, click 'OK' to close the Excel Options dialog box. Your Ribbon will now show the changes you've made.

The Quick Access Toolbar

The Quick Access Toolbar is your personal command center in Excel, always visible at the top of the application window. While it comes pre-loaded with a few basic commands like 'Save,' 'Undo,' and 'Redo,' its true potential lies in its customizability. Consider it as your personalized shortcut to Excel's extensive capabilities.

Customizing the Quick Access Toolbar

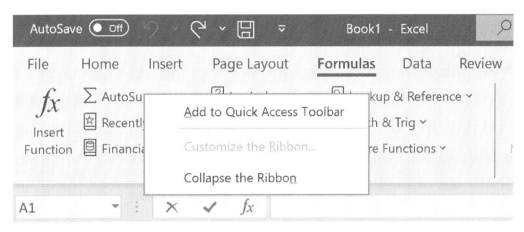

To add a command to the Quick Access Toolbar, right-click on any command from the Ribbon and choose 'Add to Quick Access Toolbar.' Alternatively, you can click the small downward arrow at the end of the Quick Access Toolbar and select 'More Commands.' This will open a dialog box where you can choose from a list of all available commands. Once you've selected the commands you want, click 'Add,' and they will appear on your Quick Access Toolbar. This is a fantastic way to keep your most frequently used or hard-to-find commands just a click away, streamlining your workflow significantly.

The Formula Bar

The Formula Bar is another essential tool in Excel, situated right above the spreadsheet grid and below the Ribbon. Whenever you click on a cell, its content—whether data or a formula—appears in the Formula Bar. This is particularly useful when you're working with cells that contain long text strings or complex formulas.

Utilizing the Formula Bar

You can directly type into the Formula Bar to enter or edit data in a cell. When working with formulas, the Formula Bar provides a clearer and more spacious area to construct and edit your calculations. As you type a formula, Excel's IntelliSense feature will offer suggestions, making it easier to complete your formula correctly. This feature proves its worth as you tackle more complex mathematical and data analysis tasks in Excel.

The Status Bar

Now, let's take a look at the Status Bar located at the very bottom of your Excel window. This is your quick-reference dashboard, providing a snapshot of various aspects of your workbook.

Customizing the Status Bar

The Status Bar can display a range of information about the cells you've selected, such as the sum, average, or count. To customize what information appears, right-click on the Status Bar and select the options you find most useful. Additionally, the Status Bar offers quick access to different view options like 'Normal,' 'Page Layout,' and 'Page Break Preview,' as well as a zoom slider to adjust the size of your worksheet on the screen.

Status Indicators

You'll also notice various status indicators like 'Ready,' 'Edit,' or 'Calculate.' These indicators give you real-time information about what Excel is currently doing. For example, 'Ready' means Excel is idle and awaiting your next command, while 'Calculate' indicates that Excel is processing a formula.

Mastering Basic Operations

Now that we've acquainted ourselves with Excel's interface, it's time to roll up our sleeves and start working with Excel worksheets. We will cover the fundamental operations of creating, saving, and opening worksheets. You'll take these fundamental steps every time you work with Excel, so let's get comfortable with them.

Creating a New Worksheet

Every great project begins with a blank slate, and in Excel, that blank slate is called a worksheet. When you open Excel, it starts with a new blank file, known as a workbook, that has one worksheet. If you need more worksheets, just click the 'New Sheet' button at the bottom of the Excel window, next to your existing worksheet tabs.

If you're wondering why you might need more than one worksheet, think of a workbook as a binder. Each worksheet in the workbook is like a separate page, allowing you to keep related information well-organized in one place.

In simple terms, a workbook is a complete file containing multiple sheets, including worksheets. A worksheet, on the other hand, is a single component within the workbook, providing a space for your data, calculations, and charts. Understanding this relationship between a workbook and its worksheets is crucial for effective data organization and manipulation in Excel.

Now that your new worksheet is set up, it's time to save your workbook.

Saving Your Progress

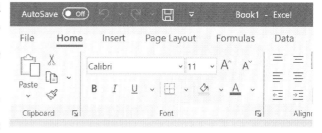

Nothing is more vital in your Excel journey than saving your work regularly. The safety net protects your work from unexpected shutdowns, power outages, or accidental window closures.

Here's how to save your work: click on the 'File' tab on the Ribbon, and then select 'Save' or 'Save As'. The 'Save' command saves the changes in the existing file, while 'Save As' lets you save the workbook in a new file or a different location.

Moreover, there's another fundamental aspect to saving - the Autosave feature. This automatic function regularly saves your progress at specified intervals. By enabling Autosave, you can reduce the risk of losing significant updates, especially when dealing with large volumes of data or complex calculations. Remember, the Autosave feature is a continuous backup of your work, helping maintain your peace of mind as you navigate through your Excel tasks.

Choosing the Right File Format

When you save your workbook, Excel offers a variety of file formats to choose from. Each file format serves a different purpose, and the right one for you depends on what you plan to do with your workbook.

- The default is '.xlsx', which is suitable for most purposes. This format supports all Excel features; you should use this unless you have a specific reason not to.

- '.xls' is the format used in older versions of Excel (2003 and earlier). Use this if you're sharing your workbook with someone who uses an older version of Excel.

- '.csv' (Comma-Separated Values) is a plain-text format used when you need to import or export a single sheet of data without any formulas or special formatting.

As we move forward, we'll come across situations where these various file formats come into play. Just keep these choices in mind, and I'll provide guidance on when to use each of them.

With our work now safely saved, let's learn how to open your workbook the next time you want to work on it.

Reopening Your Workbook

We've created our workbook, worked on our worksheet, and saved our progress. Now, it's time to close Excel. But what about when you come back later? You'll need to know how to reopen your workbook to pick up where you left off.

Here's how you do it:

   1. Launch Excel.

   2. Click on the 'File' tab in the Ribbon, and then select 'Open'.

   3. In the 'Open' dialogue box, navigate to the location where you saved your workbook.

   4. Click on the workbook, and then click 'Open'.

Voila! Your workbook opens, and you're ready to get back to work.

Excel also has a feature to quickly access recently opened workbooks. When you select 'Open' from the 'File' tab, you'll see a list of recent workbooks. If the workbook you want to open is in the list, just click on it, and you're good to go.

Data Entry Essentials

Now that we are able to create, save, and open worksheets, let's tackle one of the most important steps in our Excel course, which is data entry. After all, Excel is all about data. Whether you're building a budget, organizing a guest list, or conducting a complex statistical analysis, it all starts with entering data. Let's get to it.

Entering Text, Numbers, and Dates

In Excel, it's all about data – the essential building block of every worksheet. The types of data you'll most frequently encounter are text, numbers, and dates. To begin, let's talk about selecting a cell. A cell is the smallest unit in an Excel worksheet where you can enter data. To select a cell, move your cursor to it and click once. You'll notice that the cell is now outlined, indicating it's ready for data entry.

Select a cell by clicking on it. Then, simply type your data—whether it's text, a number, or a date—and press 'Enter.' Notice that your entry also appears in the Formula Bar as you type. This can be helpful when you're working with long strings of text or large numbers.

Selecting, Inserting, and Deleting Cells, Rows, and Columns

As you add data, you may need to modify the structure of your worksheet. Maybe you need an extra column for new data or want to remove a row of outdated information. Let's learn how to select, insert, and delete cells, rows, and columns.

To select a cell, just click on it. To select a row, click on the row number on the left, and to select a column, click on the column letter at the top. Once a row or column is selected, it's highlighted.

First, select where you want the new cell, row, or column to go to insert a new cell, row, or column. Then, right-click and select 'Insert' from the context menu. Excel will add a new cell, shift other cells down or to the right, and will add a new row or column.

The process of deleting a cell, row, or column is similar. Select the cell, row, or column you want to remove, right-click, and select 'Delete' from the context menu.

Managing Ranges

Excel isn't just about individual cells. Often, it's about how cells interact with each other in a range. A range in Excel is simply a group of cells you work with as a set. You might want to format a range of cells with the same color, calculate the sum of a range of numbers, or sort a range of rows based on one column. So, understanding how to manage ranges is essential.

Selecting a Range - First things first—how do you select a range? It's as simple as clicking and dragging. Start by clicking on the first cell of the range you want to select. Keep the mouse button pressed, drag to the range's last cell, and then release the button. When you see all the cells highlighted from the first to the last, it means that they're selected.

Entering Data in a Range - Now, what if you want to enter the same data in a whole range of cells? You don't have to enter it in each cell individually—that would be a pain. Instead, Excel allows you to enter the data once and fill the entire range with it.

Here's how to do it:

    1. Select the range you want to fill.

    2. Type the data with which you want to fill the range, but don't press 'Enter' just yet.

    3. Press 'Ctrl+Enter.'

Copying and Moving Ranges - As you work with data, you might need to copy or move ranges. You can do this easily with Excel's 'Copy' and 'Cut' commands.

To copy a range, select it, right-click, and then select 'Copy.' To paste the copied range, select the top-left cell of the range where you want to paste, right-click, and then select 'Paste.'

Moving a range is done using the same process, but this time, you'll use 'Cut' instead of 'Copy.'

Enhancing Data Entry

From importing data from multiple sources to utilizing features like Auto-fill and Flash Fill, learn how to streamline your data entry and analysis tasks.

Data Import

Excel offers various options for importing data, making it a versatile tool for data analysis and report creation. Here, I will show you the different ways in which you can insert external data into your Excel workbook.

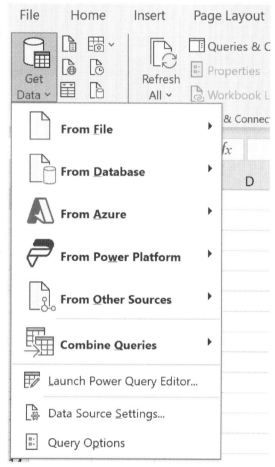

Importing from Text Files - One of the most common data sources is a text file, often in CSV (Comma-Separated Values) format. To import data from a text file, go to the 'Data' tab on the Ribbon and click on 'Get Data.' From the dropdown, select 'From Text/CSV.' Navigate to the location of your text file, select it, and click 'Import.' A preview window will appear, allowing you to specify how Excel should interpret the data, such as delimiters and data types for each column. Once you're satisfied, click 'Load,' and the data will populate a new worksheet.

Importing from Other Spreadsheets - If you have data in another Excel workbook that you'd like to use in your current workbook, you don't have to start from scratch. Go to 'Data' > 'Get Data' > 'Combine Queries' > 'Append Queries.' Here, you can select the workbook and specific worksheet you want to import. This method is particularly useful when you have similar data structures across multiple Excel files, and you want to consolidate them.

Importing from Databases - Excel also allows you to connect directly to various types of databases like SQL Server, Oracle, and others. To do this, navigate to 'Data' > 'Get Data' > 'From Database.' You'll be prompted to enter the database credentials and select the tables or queries you want to import. This feature is incredibly powerful for businesses that store data in centralized databases, as it allows for real-time data analysis without the need for manual data entry.

Importing from Online Services - In an increasingly connected world, you may find the need to import data from online services like SharePoint, Microsoft Dynamics, and even social media platforms. Excel supports this through its 'Data' > 'Get Data' > 'From Online Services' option. The steps are similar to database import but will require you to log in to the online service from which you're importing data.

Importing from the Web - Sometimes, the data you need is on a webpage. Excel has a feature for this, too! Go to 'Data' > 'Get Data' > 'From Web,' and you'll be able to enter a URL and select the specific tables you want to import into your workbook.

Data Refresh - After importing data, especially from databases or online services, you'll often have the option to 'Refresh' the data. This means you can update the data in your Excel workbook to reflect any changes in the source data, all with just a click of a button. This is found under 'Data' > 'Refresh All.'

Auto-fill Feature

One of Excel's most convenient features is the Auto-fill function, designed to save you time and effort when entering data that follows a pattern. Imagine you have a series of dates, numbers, or even text that follows a specific sequence. Instead of manually entering each cell, you can use Auto-fill to complete the series.

To use this feature, enter the first value of your series in a cell. Then, hover your mouse over the small square at the bottom-right corner of the cell (known as the "fill handle"). Click and drag it over the range where you want the series to extend. Excel will automatically fill in the cells based on the pattern it detects in your initial entries. For example, if you enter "1" in a cell and drag the fill handle, Excel will fill the cells with a series of consecutive numbers: 2, 3, 4, and so on.

You can also use Auto-fill for more complex patterns. For instance, if you enter "2" and "4" in adjacent cells and then use the Auto-fill feature, Excel will continue the pattern by filling in "6," "8," "10," etc. This feature offers remarkable versatility, capable of managing dates, weekdays, months, and even custom lists that you can define as per your preferences.

Cell Comments and Notes

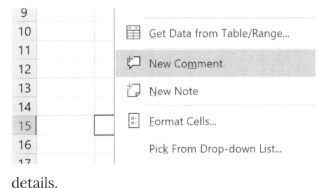

Excel is more than just a tool for numbers and formulas. It also allows you to provide context to your data, which is where cell comments and notes come in handy. By adding comments or notes to a cell, you can offer additional explanations, reminders, or context that can be really helpful when sharing spreadsheets with colleagues or simply reminding yourself of certain details.

To add a comment, right-click on the cell where you want the comment to appear and select 'New Comment.' A text box will appear where you can type your comment. Once you've entered your comment, click outside the text box to close it. A small triangle will appear in the upper-right corner of the cell to indicate that a comment has been added. Hovering over the cell will display the comment.

Notes work similarly but are a bit simpler. Right-click on the cell, choose 'Insert Note,' and then type your note. A small red square will appear in the corner of the cell to indicate that a note has been added.

Flash Fill

Flash Fill is another powerful feature in Excel that can save you a significant amount of time, especially when dealing with repetitive data entry tasks. Unlike Auto-fill, which requires you to define a pattern manually, Flash Fill automatically detects patterns in your data as you type.

As an illustration, suppose you have a column of complete names, and you want to extract only the first names into a new column. You could write a formula to do this, but with Flash Fill, all you need to do is type the first name from the first full name in the adjacent cell. As you start to type the first name from the second full name, Excel's Flash Fill will recognize the pattern and suggest filling in the rest of the first names for you. Press 'Enter,' and voila! Your new column is populated with just the first names.

To activate Flash Fill, you can either go to 'Data' > 'Flash Fill,' or you can use the keyboard shortcut Ctrl+E. It's a smart feature that learns from your actions, making it an invaluable tool for efficient data entry and manipulation.

Basic Formatting Techniques

Excel isn't just a number-crunching machine; it's also a canvas where you can bring your data to life. With the right formatting, your data becomes visually engaging and easier to read and comprehend.

So, let's take our first steps into the world of Excel aesthetics by learning about font adjustment, number formatting, cell alignment, and the use of cell styles and themes.

Adjusting Fonts

Fonts are like the clothes of your data—they give your data its appearance. Different fonts can evoke different feelings and highlight different types of information.

You'll find Excel's font options in the 'Font' group on the 'Home' tab of the Ribbon. From here, you can change the font face, adjust the size, make your text bold, italic, or underlined, and even change the color of your text.

Try to choose fonts and font styles that make your data clear and easy to read. While playing with different font styles can be fun, remember that clarity is the goal. Stick to fonts that are simple and readable, especially when you're sharing your workbook with others.

But formatting isn't just about making your data look good. It's also about making it meaningful. For that, we turn to number formats.

Applying Number Formats

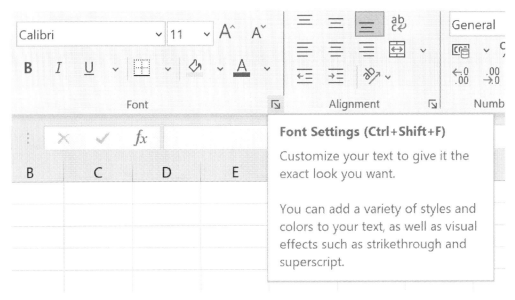

Numbers can represent many different things—currency, percentages, dates, or just plain numbers. With number formats, you can help Excel and your readers understand exactly what your numbers represent.

In the ' Number ' group, Excel's number format options are also on the 'Home' tab of the Ribbon. Here, you can format numbers as currency, apply a percentage format, indicate numbers as dates, and much more.

For instance, format your numbers as currency if you're working with prices. Excel will automatically add the currency symbol and use two decimal places. If you're working with percentages, use the percentage format.

Number formats don't just change how your numbers look; they change how Excel treats your numbers. For instance, if you format a number as a percentage, Excel will treat it as a percentage in formulas and calculations.

Of course, you can easily modify the format of any cell in Excel by right-clicking on it and selecting the "Format Cells" command from the drop-down menu.

1. *General* - The "General" format is Excel's default setting and provides a blank slate. It doesn't have any specific number format, so Excel will not add decimal places or commas automatically.

This is useful when you have a mix of different types of numerical data that don't require special formatting.

2. *Number* - The "Number" format is your go-to for most numerical values. It allows you to control the number of decimal places, use a comma as a thousand separator, and even display negative numbers in various ways (like with a minus sign, in red, or in parentheses). This format is particularly useful for financial reports and data analysis, where precision cannot be underestimated.

3. *Currency* - When dealing with monetary values, the "Currency" format becomes your most trusted ally. It automatically adds the currency symbol based on your system's regional settings. Like the "Number" format, you can control the number of decimal places and how negative numbers are displayed. The currency symbol appears right next to the first digit in the cell.

4. *Accounting* - Similar to the "Currency" format, the "Accounting" format is designed for financial statements. It aligns the currency symbols and decimal points in a column, which makes it easier to read large tables of monetary values. Unlike "Currency," the currency symbol is aligned to the left edge of the cell, and the number is aligned to the right.

5. *Date* - The "Date" format offers various ways to display dates, ranging from simple MM/DD/YYYY formats to more verbose styles that include the day of the week. This is crucial for scheduling, project planning, and any scenario where the date is a significant data point.

6. *Time* - The "Time" format allows you to display time in several ways, including both 12-hour and 24-hour formats. This is useful for anything from tracking work hours to scheduling events.

7. *Percentage* - The "Percentage" format automatically multiplies the cell's numerical value by 100 and displays it with a percent sign, which is especially advantageous when working with ratios or proportions.

8. *Fraction* - The "Fraction" format converts decimal numbers into fractions. This format can be valuable in fields like engineering, carpentry, or any situation where fractions are more meaningful than decimals.

9. *Scientific* - The "Scientific" format comes in handy for presenting numbers in scientific notation, proving exceptionally practical when dealing with large or small numbers. For example, the speed of light (299,792,458 meters per second) can be displayed as $2.99792458E+08$.

10. *Text* - The "Text" format treats the number as text, meaning it will be displayed exactly as entered. When you want to start a cell with a zero (e.g., zip codes, phone numbers) and don't want Excel to remove it, this feature proves to be quite helpful.

11. *Special* - The "Special" format includes options for formatting phone numbers, ZIP codes, and other specialized numerical data. When you're dealing with data that follows a specific structure, this format is your reliable companion.

12. *Custom* - The "Custom" format goes beyond the predefined settings, allowing you to create your own number formats. For example, you could create a custom format to display numbers as "1st," "2nd," "3rd," etc., or to display dates in a very specific way.

Aligning Cell Contents

Think of a painting with subjects placed off-center or a book where the text is misaligned—it would be challenging to appreciate, wouldn't it? The same principle applies to your data. Proper alignment of your cell contents is key to ensuring your data is easy to read and understand.

Alignment options are located in the 'Alignment' group on the 'Home' tab of the Ribbon. Here, you can align your text to the cell's left, center, or right. You can also align it to the top, middle, or bottom.

Horizontal alignment is often used to differentiate different types of data. For instance, you might align text to the left, numbers to the right, and headers to the center. Vertical alignment, on the other hand, becomes quite useful when you're working with multiple lines of text within a cell.

Using Cell Styles and Themes

Now, let's give our worksheet a touch of style. Excel provides cell styles and themes to effortlessly enhance your worksheet with just a few clicks.

Cell styles are combinations of various formatting options that you can apply all at once. They're found in the 'Styles' group on the 'Home' tab of the Ribbon. Excel provides various pre-made styles, including different fonts, number formats, colors, and borders.

For example, you might use one of Excel's 'Heading' styles for the headers in your worksheet and one of the 'Data' styles for your numbers. You can even create your own custom styles if you have specific formatting combinations you use frequently.

Themes, on the other hand, are sets of colors, fonts, and effects that give your entire workbook a consistent and professional look. You can find themes on the 'Page Layout' tab of the Ribbon.

Basic Math Operations

You've dressed up your data, aligned it perfectly, and now it's time for the grand finale of Day 1: mathematical operations. Excel is a master mathematician, ready to handle everything from simple addition to complex statistical analysis. But before we get ahead of ourselves, let's start with the basics: addition, subtraction, multiplication, and division.

Addition

Excel is excellent at addition, and it couldn't be simpler to do. All you need to do is start with an equals sign (=), followed by the numbers or cell references you want to add, with a plus sign (+) in between.

For example, to add the numbers 2 and 3, you would type **=2+3** into a cell and press 'Enter'. Excel will calculate the result and display **5** in the cell. If you want to add the values in cells A1 and A2, you will type **=A1+A2**.

And what if you have a range of cells you want to sum up? That's where the **SUM** function comes into action. For instance, you'd type =SUM(A1:A10) to add all the numbers from A1 to A10.

Subtraction

Subtraction is equally simple. Replace the plus sign (+) with a minus sign (-); you're subtracting instead of adding. So **=5-2** gives you **3**, and **=A2-A1** gives you the difference between the values in cells A2 and A1.

Keep in mind that Excel performs these operations in the order of operations (parentheses, exponents, multiplication and division from left to right, addition and subtraction from left to right), not from left to right. If you want to ensure Excel performs operations in a specific order, use parentheses. For example, **=(2+3)*5** gives you **25**, not **17**.

Multiplication

When it comes to multiplication, Excel swaps out the x for an asterisk (*). So **=2*3** gives you **6**, and **=A1*A2** multiplies the values in cells A1 and A2.

And if you want to multiply a series of numbers together, you can use the **PRODUCT** function. So **=PRODUCT(A1:A10)** will result in multiplying all the numbers from A1 to A10.

Division

Division in Excel uses the forward slash (/). So to divide 6 by 2, you'd type **=6/2** and get **3**, and **=A2/A1** divides the value in cell A2 by the value in A1.

Be careful with division in Excel, though. If you try to divide by zero, Excel will give you a **#DIV/0! Error**. This is Excel's way of telling you that something's gone wrong. So always make sure you're not trying to divide by zero; if you're dividing by a cell reference, make sure that cell doesn't have zero.

Applying Math Operations to Real-World Tasks

We've gone through the fundamental mathematical operations, but what does this look like in a practical scenario? Let's say you're planning a birthday party. You have a list of costs—cake, decorations, party favors—and you want to determine the total cost and how much you'll need per guest.

You'd enter each cost in a cell, then use the **SUM** function to add up the costs and find the total. Then, you'd divide the total cost by the number of guests to determine how much you need per guest.

It might look something like this:

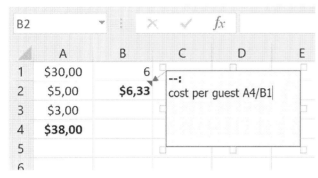

In cell A1, you'd enter the cost of the cake.

In cell A2, the cost of the decorations.

In cell A3, the cost of party favors.

In cell A4, you'd enter =**SUM(A1:A3)** to find the total cost.

- In cell B1, you'd enter the number of guests.

- In cell B2, you'd enter =**A4/B1** to find the cost per guest.

Now you have a total budget and know how much to ask each guest if you split the cost. All thanks to some simple math operations in Excel!

Chapter Two

DAY 2: FORMULAS AND FUNCTIONS

If we were to compare Excel to a car, formulas and functions would be its engine. They're the powerhouse that enables you to conduct calculations, analyze data, and automate tasks, effectively transforming a basic spreadsheet into a dynamic and robust tool for data analysis.

But, why are formulas and functions so crucial? Well, they save you time and effort by doing the heavy lifting for you. Instead of manually calculating the sum or average of a column of numbers, a simple formula can do it in a fraction of a second. Need to make a decision based on data? Logical functions like IF, AND, and OR can help you set conditions and make those decisions automatically.

Today, we'll start by understanding the syntax and usage of Excel formulas, which is like learning the basic grammar of a new language. Once you grasp this, you'll find it much easier to communicate what you want Excel to do for you.

Next, we'll take a look at some of the most commonly used functions like SUM, AVERAGE, COUNT, MIN, and MAX. These are the building blocks that you'll use over and over again, regardless of your project.

I'll also introduce you to logical functions, which allow you to add decision-making capabilities to your spreadsheets. This is especially useful for tasks like categorizing data or making calculations based on specific conditions.

As we progress, I'll touch upon some advanced functions that offer even more flexibility and power. I'll also help you understand the importance of relative and absolute cell references, a concept that will assist you in creating more versatile formulas. Finally, remember that no one is perfect, and errors do happen. That's why we'll wrap up the day by learning about error handling in formulas so that you can troubleshoot issues like a pro.

By the conclusion of this chapter, you'll have gained a strong grasp of utilizing formulas and functions to enhance your workflow and maximize the value of your data.

Understanding Excel Formulas: Syntax and Usage

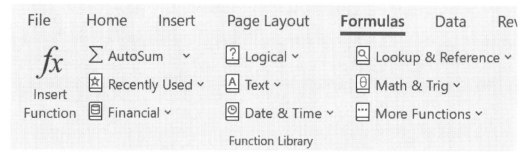

Excel formulas are the core foundation of any spreadsheet, empowering you to perform calculations, analyze data, and automate tasks. Comprehending the syntax and application of Excel formulas is vital for those seeking to unlock the complete potential of this software. Below, I'll break down the key components of Excel formulas and how to use them effectively.

Basic Syntax

The basic syntax of an Excel formula starts with an equal sign (=), followed by the function name (e.g., SUM, AVERAGE), and then the arguments within parentheses. For example: **=SUM(A1:A5)**

The Equal Sign (=) - The equal sign is the initial character that tells Excel you're about to enter a formula, not just data or text.

- *Placement*: It must be the first character in the cell where you're entering the formula.
- *Exceptions*: If you start a cell with a different character, Excel will treat the content as text or data, not a formula.

Function Name - This specifies what kind of calculation or operation you want to perform. Excel has a wide range of built-in functions for various purposes like mathematical operations, text manipulation, and data analysis.

- *Case Sensitivity*: Excel functions are not case-sensitive. **SUM**, **Sum**, and **sum** are all treated the same.
- *Auto-suggest Feature*: As you start typing a function name, Excel will show a drop-down list of functions that match the entered text. You can select from this list to auto-complete the function name.
- *Function Wizard*: You can also use the Function Wizard (accessed by pressing **Shift + F3** or clicking the **fx** button near the formula bar) to search for functions and see their descriptions.

Arguments

Arguments are the specific data points or ranges the function will act upon. They are enclosed in parentheses immediately following the function name.

- *Single vs. Multiple Arguments*: Some functions require only one argument, while others may require multiple. When using multiple arguments, separate them with commas.
  - Single Argument: **=SQRT(16)**
  - Multiple Arguments: **=SUM(A1, A2, A3)**
- *Dynamic Arguments*: You can also use other functions, constants, or formulas as arguments.
  - Example: **=SUM(A1, AVERAGE(B1:B3), 10)**
- *Optional Arguments*: Some functions have optional arguments, which are enclosed in square brackets in the function's tooltip.
  - Example: **=VLOOKUP(A1, B1:C10, 2, [FALSE])**
- *Data Types*: Make sure to use the correct data type for each argument. For example, text should be enclosed in quotation marks.
  - Example: **=IF(A1 > 10, "Greater", "Smaller")**

Types of Functions

Excel offers a lot of functions to cater to various needs, from basic calculations to complex data analysis. Below, you will learn about the different types of functions in more detail.

Mathematical functions are used for performing basic to advanced mathematical calculations.

Common Functions: **SUM, AVERAGE, MIN, MAX, SQRT**, etc.

Example: **=AVERAGE(C2:C6)**

This formula calculates the average of the values in cells C2 through C6.

Logical functions allow you to make decisions based on conditions, essentially introducing "if-then-else" logic into your spreadsheets.

Common Functions: **IF, AND, OR, NOT, XOR**

Example: **=IF(A1>10, "Yes", "No")**

This formula checks if the value in cell A1 is greater than 10. If it is, the formula returns "Yes"; otherwise, it returns "No".

Text functions help you manipulate and manage text data in various ways.

Common Functions: **CONCATENATE** (or **CONCAT** in newer versions), **LEFT, RIGHT, MID, UPPER, LOWER**, etc.

Example: **=CONCATENATE(A1, " ", B1)**

This formula combines the text in cells A1 and B1, separated by a space.

Lookup functions enable you to search for specific data within a table or range and return corresponding values.

Common Functions: **VLOOKUP, HLOOKUP, INDEX, MATCH**

Example: **=VLOOKUP(A1, C1:D10, 2, FALSE)**

This formula searches for the value in cell A1 within the first column of the range C1:D10 and returns the corresponding value from the second column.

Date and Time Functions functions assist you in working with date and time data, allowing you to perform calculations or conversions.

- Common Functions: **NOW**, **TODAY**, **YEAR**, **MONTH**, **DAY**, **HOUR**, **MINUTE**, etc.
- Example: =**TODAY()**

This formula returns the current date.

Operators

Operators are used to perform basic arithmetic operations and can be combined with functions for more intricate calculations.

Common Operators:

- Addition (+)
- Subtraction (-)
- Multiplication (*)
- Division (/)
- Exponentiation (^)

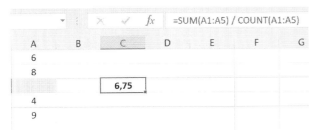

Example: =**SUM(A1:A5) / COUNT(A1:A5)**

This formula calculates the average of the values in cells A1 through A5 by summing them up and then dividing by the count of non-empty cells.

Nesting Functions

Nesting functions means placing one function inside another, allowing you to perform more complex operations that require multiple steps.

How to Nest: To nest functions, you place one function within the parentheses of another.

Example: =**IF(AND(A1>10, B1<5), "Yes", "No")**

This formula uses the **AND** function inside the **IF** function. It checks if the value in cell A1 is greater than 10 and the value in cell B1 is less than 5. If both conditions are met, it returns "Yes"; otherwise, it returns "No."

Best Practices

Mastering Excel is not just about knowing the functions and syntax; it's also about adhering to best practices that make your work more efficient, understandable, and error-free. Below are some best practices you should consider when working with Excel formulas.

Comments serve as annotations within your worksheet to explain what a particular formula does, especially if it's complex or not self-explanatory.

- How to Add: To insert a comment in a cell, select the cell and press **Shift + F2**. Alternatively, you can right-click on the cell and choose "Insert Comment."

- Why Use Them: Comments are particularly useful for team projects or for worksheets that you'll revisit after a long time. They act as in-sheet documentation that can save you and others a lot of time.

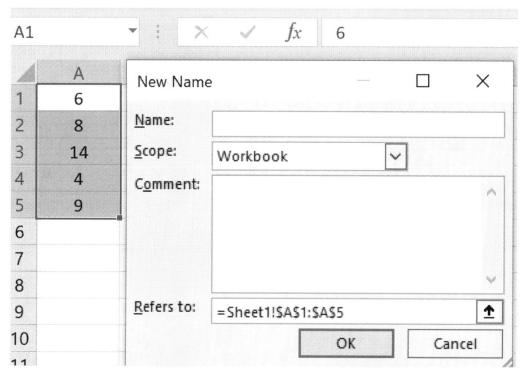

Naming ranges means assigning a name to a particular range of cells, making your formulas easier to read and manage.

How to Name a Range? Select the range of cells, go to the "Formulas" tab, and choose "Define Name" or simply type the name into the Name Box next to the formula bar.

Benefits:

- Increases readability: **=SUM(SalesData)** is easier to understand than **=SUM(A1:A10)**.

- Simplifies navigation: Named ranges make finding and selecting specific elements easier.

- Enhances accuracy: Reduces the risk of selecting the wrong cell range.

Error Checking - Excel provides error messages like **#VALUE!** or **#DIV/0!** to indicate that something is wrong with your formula.

Common Error Types:

- **#VALUE!**: Incorrect data type
- **#DIV/0!**: Division by zero
- **#NAME?**: Excel doesn't recognize text in the formula
- **#N/A**: Value not available

How to Debug:

- Use Excel's built-in "Error Checking" feature under the "Formulas" tab.
- Hover over the error cell to see an explanation and suggested actions.
- Manually inspect the formula and the referenced cells.

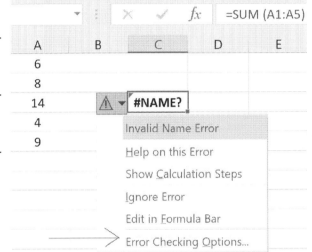

Relative and Absolute Cell References

One of Excel's core features is the ability to reference cells in formulas. To make the most of Excel, it's crucial to understand the difference between relative and absolute cell references. These two reference types behave differently when copied and pasted into new cells, and knowing when to use each can save you considerable time and effort.

Before getting to the specifics, it's essential to understand what a cell reference is. In Excel, a cell reference identifies the unique column and row location of a cell, such as A1, B2, or C3. These references are used in formulas to perform calculations, look up values, and more.

Relative Cell References

Relative cell references are the default type in Excel and are probably what you encounter most often. They are called "relative" because they change, or "adjust," relative to their position when you copy them to another cell. This feature is convenient for applying the same formula across multiple rows or columns quickly.

Syntax: a relative cell reference is simply the column letter and row number without any special characters—for instance, **A1**.

Now consider this example: Imagine you have a list of numbers in column A (from A1 to A5), and you want to add 10 to each number. You could write the formula **=A1+10** in cell B1 and then copy it down to B5. Excel will automatically adjust the formula to **=A2+10**, **=A3+10**, and so on.

Absolute Cell References

Absolute cell references become important when you need a cell reference to remain unaltered, even after copying the formula to a different cell. This is especially valuable when you have a consistent value that you intend to utilize in multiple calculations.

Syntax: an absolute cell reference is denoted by a **$** symbol before the column letter and row number, like **A1**.

Example: Suppose you have a tax rate in cell C1 that you want to apply to a list of prices in column A (from A1 to A5). You could use the formula **=A1*C1** in cell B1. When you copy this formula down to B5, the reference to C1 remains constant, ensuring that the same tax rate is applied to all prices.

Mixed Cell References

Mixed cell references are a hybrid of relative and absolute references. In a mixed reference, one part (either the row or the column) is absolute, and the other is relative.

- **Absolute Column, Relative Row**: $A1
- **Relative Column, Absolute Row**: A$1

Mixed references can be helpful when you want only the row or column to adjust when copying the formula. For example, you might want to multiply values across a row by a single value in a column or vice versa.

Understanding the nuances between relative, absolute, and mixed cell references can significantly improve your efficiency in Excel. Relative references are great for applying the same formula across multiple cells with varying data, while absolute references are ideal for using a constant value in multiple calculations. Mixed references offer the best of both worlds, allowing for flexible yet controlled calculations.

Common Excel Functions: SUM, AVERAGE, COUNT, MIN, MAX

As I mentioned, Excel provides a wide array of functions to handle a multitude of tasks, spanning from basic arithmetic to complex data analysis. Below are some of the most commonly used Excel functions, along with their syntax, examples, and use-cases.

SUM Function

The SUM function is a foundational tool in numerous applications, including financial modeling, budgeting, and accounting. Its primary role is to sum up all the numbers in a given range or list, making it one of Excel's most frequently utilized functions.

Syntax: **=SUM(number1, [number2], ...)**

Example: **=SUM(A1:A5)** or **=SUM(A1, B1, C1)**

Additional Points

- Multiple Ranges: The function allows for the summing of multiple ranges, like =SUM(A1:A5, C1:C5).

- Negative Numbers: It also accounts for negative numbers in the sum.

- Text and Blank Cells: The function ignores the text and blank cells.

- Dynamic Updates: The SUM function will automatically update the result if the numbers in the targeted cells change.

AVERAGE Function

The AVERAGE function is commonly employed in statistical analyses, grading systems, and performance metrics. It calculates the mean of a set of numbers, offering a quick way to understand the central tendency of a data set.

Syntax: **=AVERAGE(number1, [number2], ...)**

Example: **=AVERAGE(A1:A5)** or **=AVERAGE(A1, B1, C1)**

Additional Points

- Ignoring Non-Numeric Cells: The function automatically excludes cells containing text or that are empty.

- Zero Inclusion: Unlike other functions like COUNT, AVERAGE includes zeros in its calculations.

- Weighted Average: For a weighted average, you can use **=SUMPRODUCT(A1:A5, B1:B5) / SUM(B1:B5)**.

- Dynamic Behavior: Like the SUM function, AVERAGE also updates automatically when the data in the targeted cells change.

COUNT Function

The COUNT function is used when you need to quickly assess the size of a dataset, specifically the number of cells that contain numerical values. This function is frequently applied in inventory management, data validation, and statistical analysis.

Syntax: **=COUNT(value1, [value2], ...)**

Example: **=COUNT(A1:A5)** or **=COUNT(A1, B1, C1)**

Additional Points

- Excludes Text and Empty Cells: The function will not count cells that are empty or contain text.

- Multiple Ranges: You can count across multiple ranges, like **=COUNT(A1:A5, C1:C5)**.

- Dynamic Updates: The result will automatically update if the numbers in the targeted cells change.

MIN Function

When you need to identify the smallest value within a dataset, you can count on this function. You can use this function to find the lowest score, the least amount of time taken, or the smallest expense.

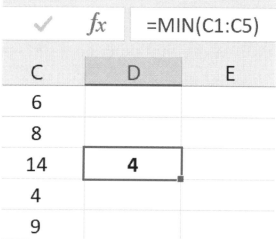

Syntax: **=MIN(number1, [number2], ...)**

Example: **=MIN(A1:A5)** or **=MIN(A1, B1, C1)**

Additional Points

- Text and Empty Cells: The function ignores cells that contain text or are empty.

- Negative Numbers: The function considers negative numbers, so if your range includes negative values, MIN will return the smallest among them.

- Multiple Ranges: Like COUNT, you can also find the minimum value across multiple ranges, like **=MIN(A1:A5, C1:C5)**.

MAX Function

The MAX function is equally important, especially when you're interested in identifying the highest value in a dataset, which could be the highest sales in a month, the maximum temperature, or the largest expense incurred.

Syntax: **=MAX(number1, [number2], ...)**

Example: **=MAX(A1:A5) or =MAX(A1, B1, C1)**

Additional Points

- Ignores Text and Empty Cells: Similar to the MIN function, MAX also ignores cells that are empty or contain text.

- Negative Numbers: If your dataset includes negative numbers, MAX will consider them and return the largest value.

- Multiple Ranges: You can find the maximum value across multiple ranges, like **=MAX(A1:A5, C1:C5)**.

Tips for Using These Functions

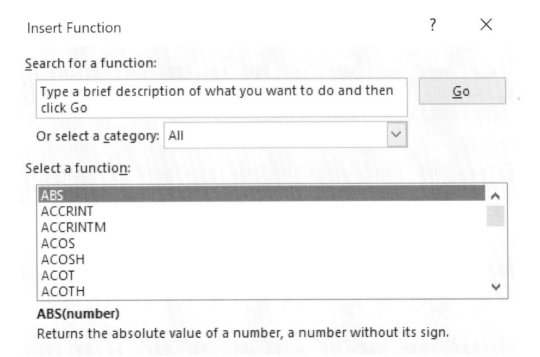

Here, I have provided some helpful tips to enhance your use of these functions:

Range Selection - When specifying cells for any of these functions, you can either manually enter each cell reference separated by commas, such as **=SUM(A1, B1, C1)**, or you can select a range of cells, like **=SUM(A1:A5)**. Using a range is particularly useful when you're working with large datasets.

Combining Functions - These functions can be combined with other Excel functions and operators for more complex calculations. For example, **=SUM(A1:A5) / COUNT(A1:A5)** calculates the average of a range of numbers. Similarly, you could find the average of the smallest and largest numbers in a range with **=(MIN(A1:A5) + MAX(A1:A5)) / 2**.

Auto-fill - After entering a function in one cell, you can easily apply it to adjacent cells. Just drag the fill handle (the small square at the bottom-right corner of the cell outline) to populate other cells in the column or row. This feature is a significant time-saver, especially when dealing with extensive data.*Function Wizard* - If you ever find yourself uncertain about a function's syntax or parameters, Excel's Function Wizard is there to help. Click on the "fx" button next to the formula bar for guided assistance. For those who are just getting started with Excel or for anyone dealing with an unfamiliar function, this tool can be a real lifesaver.

Introduction to Logical Functions: IF, AND, OR

Excel's logical functions, namely IF, AND, and OR, are powerful tools that allow you to make decisions based on conditions, thus adding a layer of intelligence to your spreadsheets.

IF Function

The IF function in Excel is a key player in making decisions within your spreadsheets. It allows you to set up conditional statements that can automate certain aspects of data analysis and presentation. Essentially, the IF function evaluates a condition and, depending on whether that condition is true or false, returns a corresponding value.

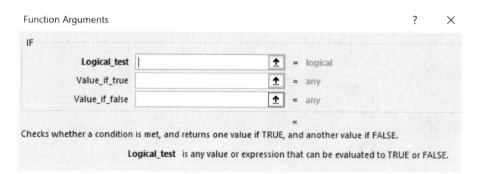

Imagine you're managing a sales team, and you want to automatically categorize sales as either "High" or "Low" based on a revenue threshold. You could use the IF function to do this. If the revenue in cell A1 is greater than $10,000, the function would return "High"; otherwise, it would return "Low."

Syntax: **=IF(logical_test, value_if_true, value_if_false)**

- logical_test: This is the condition that you want to evaluate. It could be a comparison between cell values, numbers, or even the result of other functions.

- value_if_true: This is the value that the function will return if the logical test evaluates to true.

- value_if_false: This is the value that the function will return if the logical test evaluates to false.

Example: **=IF(A1 > 10, "Yes", "No")**

In this example, the function checks if the value in cell A1 is greater than 10. If it is, the function returns "Yes"; otherwise, it returns "No."

You can also nest multiple IF functions within each other to handle more than two conditions.

For example: **=IF(A1 > 10, "More than 10", IF(A1 > 5, "Between 6 and 10", "5 or less"))**

In this nested example, the function first checks if the value in A1 is greater than 10. If it is, it returns "More than 10". If not, it moves on to the next IF function, which checks if the value is greater than 5.

AND Function

The AND function in Excel is a powerful tool for evaluating multiple conditions at once. When you need to ensure that several criteria are met before taking a specific action or returning a particular value, you can use the AND function. The AND function will return TRUE only if all the conditions specified are met; otherwise, it returns FALSE.

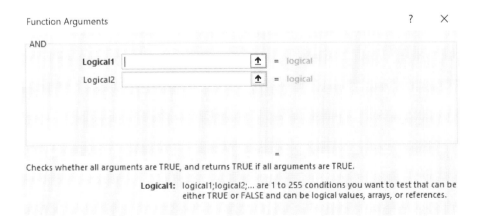

Let's say you're a project manager, and you want to flag tasks that are both overdue and high-priority. You could use the AND function to check both conditions: whether the due date has passed and whether the priority level is set to "High." The function will only return TRUE when both conditions are met, making it a convenient tool for promptly identifying tasks that demand immediate attention.

Syntax: **=AND(logical1, [logical2], ...)**

logical1, logical2, ...: These are the conditions you want to evaluate. You can include up to 255 conditions, and all must be met for the function to return TRUE.

Example: **=AND(A1 > 10, B1 < 5)**

In this example, the function will return TRUE only if the value in cell A1 is greater than 10 and the value in cell B1 is less than 5. If either of these conditions is not met, the function will return FALSE.

The AND function is often used in combination with the IF function to perform actions based on multiple conditions. For example: **=IF(AND(A1 > 10, B1 < 5), "Yes", "No")**

Here, the IF function will return "Yes" only if both conditions within the AND function are met; otherwise, it will return "No."

OR Function

This function is the flexible evaluator for multiple conditions. Unlike the AND function, which requires all conditions to be true, the OR function returns TRUE if any of the specified conditions are met. This makes it ideal for scenarios where you have multiple acceptable criteria.

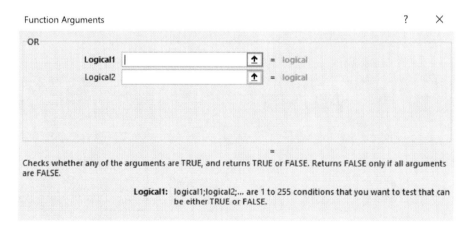

Consider this scenario: You're an event organizer, and you want to offer a discount to either returning customers or those who are buying more than five tickets. You could use the OR function to identify either of these conditions. If either condition is met, the function will return TRUE, and the discount can be applied.

Syntax: **=OR(logical1, [logical2], ...)**

logical1, logical2, ...: These are the conditions you want to evaluate. You can include up to 255 conditions, and only one needs to be met for the function to return TRUE.

Example: **=OR(A1 > 10, B1 < 5)**

In this example, the function will return TRUE if either the value in cell A1 is greater than 10 or the value in cell B1 is less than 5. If neither condition is met, the function will return FALSE.

Logical functions like AND, OR, and IF can be combined to create more sophisticated logical conditions in your Excel spreadsheets. For instance, you can nest the OR function within an IF function to perform actions based on multiple acceptable conditions. Here's how you can do it:

=IF(OR(A1 > 10, B1 < 5), "Yes", "No")

In this example, the IF function will return "Yes" if any of the conditions within the OR function are met; otherwise, it will return "No."

Advanced Functions

Advanced functions such as SUMIFS, COUNTIFS, and Array Formulas can substantially boost your data analysis capabilities in Excel. While they may seem daunting at first, understanding their syntax and practical applications can make your work much more insightful.

SUMIFS: Conditional Summation

The SUMIFS function allows you to sum values based on multiple conditions. The syntax for SUMIFS is:

=SUMIFS(sum_range, criteria_range1, criteria1, [criteria_range2, criteria2], ...)

- sum_range: The range of cells you want to sum.
- criteria_range1, criteria_range2, ...: The ranges to apply the criteria against.
- criteria1, criteria2, ...: The conditions to be met.

Example: Suppose you have a table of sales data, and you want to find the total sales for a specific product in a specific region.

To find the total sales for "Apple" in the "East" region, you would use:

=SUMIFS(C2:C5, A2:A5, "East", B2:B5, "Apple")

The result would be 300.

COUNTIFS: Conditional Counting

The COUNTIFS function counts the number of cells that meet multiple conditions. The syntax is similar to SUMIFS:

=COUNTIFS(criteria_range1, criteria1, [criteria_range2, criteria2], ...)

Example: Using the same sales data table, if you want to count the number of sales records for "Apple" in the "East" region, you would use:

=COUNTIFS(A2:A5, "East", B2:B5, "Apple")

The result would be 2.

Array Formulas: Complex Calculations

Array formulas allow you to perform multiple calculations on one or more items in an array. Array formulas can be both simple and complex. They become especially valuable when you need to extend a formula that works with a single cell to multiple cells.

Example - To square the numbers in a range (A1:A3) and sum them up, you can use an array formula:

=SUM(A1:A3^2)

To enter an array formula, you need to press Ctrl+Shift+Enter.

Error Handling in Formulas

Even the most well-crafted Excel sheet is not immune to errors. In this section, I will provide a detailed overview of error handling in Excel, from identifying common error types to implementing best practices for debugging and prevention.

Common Error Types in Excel

Before we get into the nitty-gritty of error handling, it's essential to recognize the types of errors you might come across. Here are some of the most common:

- **#DIV/0!**: Occurs when a number is divided by zero.
- **#VALUE!**: Appears when a formula receives an incompatible data type.
- **#REF!**: Indicates a reference to a non-existent cell or range.
- **#NAME?**: Occurs when Excel doesn't recognize text in a formula.
- **#N/A**: Appears when a value is not available to a function or formula.
- **#NUM!**: Occurs when a formula produces a number too large or too small to be repre-

sented in Excel.

- **#NULL!**: Appears when you specify an intersection of two areas that do not intersect.

Debugging Errors

One of the first steps in debugging errors in Excel is to understand how cells are interconnected. Excel's **Trace Precedents** and **Trace Dependents** features are invaluable for this.

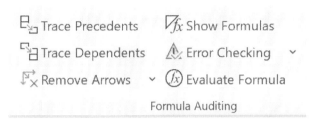

Trace Precedents: This feature shows arrows pointing from the cells that the selected cell depends on. If you have a formula in cell **C1** that uses the values in **A1** and **B1**, tracing precedents for **C1** will show arrows from **A1** and **B1** to **C1**.

Trace Dependents: This is the opposite of Trace Precedents. It shows arrows pointing to the cells that depend on the selected cell. For example, if cell **C1** depends on **A1**, tracing dependents for **A1** will show an arrow pointing to **C1**.

These features can be useful when you're dealing with complex worksheets where it's not immediately obvious how cells are related. They can aid you in quickly identifying the source of an error.

The **Evaluate Formula dialog box** is another powerful tool for debugging. It allows you to step through a formula piece by piece, evaluating each part individually. This is particularly effective for complex formulas where multiple functions and operators are used. By breaking down the formula into its constituent parts, you can isolate the specific element causing the error.

Excel's built-in **Error Checking tool** is designed to automatically identify errors in your worksheets. When activated, it scans for errors and flags them with a small triangle in the corner of the cell. Clicking on this triangle will open a dropdown menu that provides options for correcting the error or getting more information about it. This tool can be a lifesaver for large spreadsheets where manually checking each formula would be impractical.

Handling Errors Using Functions

Excel provides a variety of functions specifically designed to handle errors in formulas. These include:

- **IFERROR**: This function is a catch-all for errors. It returns a custom message or value if the formula it wraps around results in an error. For example, =**IFERROR(A1/B1, "Not Applicable")** would return "Not Applicable" if **B1** is zero, avoiding the **#DIV/0!** error.

- **ISERR** and **ISERROR**: These functions are used to check if a cell or formula results in an error. **ISERR** returns TRUE for all error types except **#N/A**, while **ISERROR** returns TRUE for all error types, including **#N/A**.

- **NA()**: This function is employed to deliberately return a **#N/A** error, which can be used to mark data that is currently unavailable or should be ignored.

Let's look at a real-world example. Suppose you're calculating the average price of items sold, but some cells in the "Price" column are empty or have text values. You could use a combination of **IFERROR** and **AVERAGE** to handle this:

=IFERROR(AVERAGE(A1:A10), "Data Incomplete")

This formula will return the average of numbers in the range **A1:A10** and will display "Data Incomplete" if any cell in the range contains an error.

Here are some best practices to ensure that your spreadsheets remain error-free and easy to manage.

Comments for Annotation - Complex formulas can quickly become challenging to understand, especially if you're revisiting a spreadsheet after some time or sharing it with others. Adding comments to cells containing complex formulas can provide context and make it easier to understand what the formula is supposed to do. To add a comment, simply select the cell and press **Shift + F2**. This is a simple yet effective way to document your work and make it more accessible to others.

Naming Ranges - Excel allows you to name ranges of cells. Named ranges can make formulas easier to read and understand. For example, instead of using =**AVERAGE(A1:A10)**, you could name the range **A1:A10** as SalesData and then use =**AVERAGE(SalesData)**. This makes it immediately clear what the formula is calculating, and it also makes debugging easier. To name a range, select the cells, right-click, and choose the "Define Name" option.

Data Validation - Data validation is a powerful feature in Excel that allows you to set restrictions on what kind of data can be entered into a cell. For example, you can set a cell to only accept numerical values, or restrict it to a list of predefined options. This can prevent many common errors, such as **#VALUE!** Errors that occur when a formula expects a number but finds text instead. To set up data validation, select the cell or range of cells, go to the Data tab, and choose Data Validation.

Auditing - Even with the best preventive measures, errors can still occur. Regular auditing of your spreadsheets can help catch these errors before they become a problem. This can be done manually by going through the spreadsheet and checking formulas and data, or you can use specialized auditing software designed to automatically detect errors and inconsistencies. Some software even provides features like formula tracing and cell dependency mapping, making it easier to identify the root cause of any errors.

Chapter Three

DAY 3: DATA MANAGEMENT

Data management is more than just a set of skills; it's an essential component in the decision-making process for businesses, researchers, and even individuals. Poorly managed data can lead to incorrect conclusions, missed opportunities, and, ultimately, a waste of time and resources. On the other hand, well-managed data can provide insights that drive innovation, improve efficiency, and create a competitive edge. Therefore, if you've ever wondered how to turn a chaotic spreadsheet into a well-organized masterpiece, this chapter is your roadmap.

We'll kick things off with sorting and filtering—two indispensable techniques that will revolutionize how you view and interact with data. Next, I'll introduce you to the magic of conditional formatting, a feature that will add a visual layer to your data analysis.

But that's not all. I'll also guide you through the challenges of managing large datasets by demonstrating how to remove duplicates and validate your data. I'll expand your knowledge with essential text functions like LEFT, RIGHT, MID, CONCATENATE, and TEXT. And let's not overlook Date and Time Functions, which will empower you to effortlessly manipulate temporal data.

Sorting and Filtering Data

In Excel, the ability to sort and filter data is not just a convenience—it's a necessity. These foundational tools enable you to make sense of the information you're working with, transforming a jumble of numbers and text into a coherent and insightful narrative. Let's discover these two crucial techniques, learning about their functionalities, applications, and the transformative impact they can have on your data management skills.

Sorting is the process of arranging your data in a specific order, be it ascending or descending, alphabetical or numerical. Think of it as tidying up your digital workspace. Just as you wouldn't want to sift through a disorganized drawer to find a single item, you wouldn't want to scroll endlessly through a spreadsheet to locate a specific piece of data.

How to Sort: A Step-by-Step Guide

Sorting data in Excel is a simple yet powerful operation. Here's a breakdown of the process:

1. *Select the Range*: First, highlight the range of cells you want to sort. This could be a single column, multiple columns, or even specific rows within a column.

2. *Navigate to the Data Tab*: Once your range is selected, go to the 'Data' tab located on the Excel ribbon at the top of your screen.

3. *Basic Sorting*: For quick sorting, you'll find two primary options:

    - Sort A to Z: This sorts the selected data in ascending order, whether it's numerical or alphabetical.

    - Sort Z to A: This sorts the data in descending order.

4. *Custom Sort*: For more nuanced sorting needs, click on the 'Sort' button to open the 'Sort Dialog Box'. Here you can:

    - Sort by Multiple Columns: You can add layers to your sorting by choosing more than one column to sort by. When you have multiple variables that need to be organized, you can use this.

    - Sort by Cell Color or Font Color: If you've color-coded your data, Excel allows you to sort by cell or font color.

- Sort by Custom Lists: If you have categories that don't follow alphabetical or numerical order (e.g., High, Medium, Low), you can create a custom list to sort them.

5. *Confirm and Apply*: Once you've made your selections, click 'OK' to apply the sort.

Why Sort? The Strategic Importance

Sorting is not just an aesthetic choice; it serves several practical purposes, especially when you're dealing with voluminous datasets. Here are some examples of when sorting can be very useful:

- *Quick Data Retrieval*: If you're a sales manager overseeing hundreds or even thousands of transactions, sorting the data by customer name or transaction date can help you quickly locate specific entries.

- *Trend Identification*: Sorting can help you spot trends that may not be immediately obvious. For example, sorting sales data by product type might show that a particular item is performing exceptionally well or poorly.

- *Data Cleaning*: Before diving into more complex analyses, sorting your data can help you identify errors or inconsistencies, such as duplicate entries or missing values.

- *Preparation for Further Analysis*: Many advanced data analysis techniques require your data to be sorted in a particular way. For instance, if you're planning to run statistical tests, you might need to sort your data in ascending or descending order.

- *Enhanced Reporting*: When presenting your findings, sorted data can make your reports easier to read and interpret, thus making your communication more effective.

Combining Sorting and Filtering

While sorting and filtering are powerful tools on their own, combining them elevates your data analysis to a whole new level. This integrated approach allows you to sift through large datasets with multiple variables, enabling you to focus on specific subsets of data and then organize them in a meaningful way.

Practical Example: Healthcare Analysis

Here's a real-world example that demonstrates the value of sorting large datasets: Imagine you're a healthcare analyst working with a dataset that contains a wealth of patient information, including age, medical history, and dates of check-ups. Your task is to identify older patients who haven't had a check-up in a while.

Step 1: Filtering by Age

- Navigate to the column that contains the patients' ages.
- Use the 'Filter' option to display only the records of patients who are over the age of 50.

Step 2: Sorting by Last Check-Up Date

- With the filtered data still on display, go to the column that shows the date of the last check-up.
- Use the 'Sort' function to organize this filtered list in ascending order based on the date. This will show you the patients who have gone the longest without a check-up at the top of the list.

By first filtering the data to only show patients over 50 and then sorting these results by the date of their last check-up, you've performed a more nuanced analysis. This targeted approach helps you:

- *Prioritize Patient Outreach*: Knowing who hasn't had a check-up in a while allows the healthcare provider to focus their outreach efforts more effectively.
- *Resource Allocation*: This information can unlock critical insights for healthcare administrators looking to allocate resources more efficiently, such as scheduling staff or planning clinics.
- *Risk Assessment*: Older patients who haven't had a recent check-up might be at higher risk for undiagnosed health issues. Your analysis could be the first step in a chain of actions that leads to early intervention and better patient outcomes.

Advanced Techniques

For those looking to go even further, Excel offers advanced filtering options like 'Top 10' or 'Bottom 10,' which can be combined with sorting for even more specialized analyses. For example, you could filter to show only the 'Top 10' oldest patients and then sort them by the number of visits they've had in the past year, revealing those who may require more immediate attention.

Introduction to Conditional Formatting

Conditional Formatting is a feature in Excel that allows you to automatically apply specific formatting—such as colors, fonts, and borders—to cells that meet certain conditions. This tool transforms your spreadsheet from a static table into a dynamic and visually compelling dashboard, making it easier to spot trends, identify outliers, and understand your data at a glance.

The primary advantage of using Conditional Formatting is its ability to make large datasets more manageable and insightful. When you're dealing with hundreds or even thousands of rows and columns, it can be challenging to focus on the data that truly matters. Conditional Formatting helps you highlight key information, making it easier to analyze and interpret your data.

Basic Types of Conditional Formatting

1. *Highlight Cell Rules*: This is the simplest type of conditional formatting. You can highlight cells based on their values, whether they are greater than, less than, or equal to a specific number.

    - Example: If you're tracking monthly sales, you could set a rule to highlight any cell with a value over $10,000 in green and any cell under $5,000 in red.

2. *Data Bars or Color Scales*: These options allow you to apply a gradient of colors to a range of cells based on their values, offering a quick way to visualize data distribution.

    - Example: In a dataset of student grades, you could use color scales to show a gradient from green (high grades) to red (low grades).

3. *Icon Sets*: These add icons next to your data points, providing a more graphical representation of your data's status.

    - Example: In a project timeline, you could use flag icons to indicate tasks that are completed, in progress, or not started.

How to Apply Conditional Formatting

1. Select the Range: Choose the cells you want to format.

2. Navigate to the 'Home' Tab: Go to the 'Conditional Formatting' option in the 'Styles' group.

3. Choose the Rule: Select the type of rule you want to apply from the dropdown menu.

4. Set the Criteria: Depending on the rule, you'll need to specify the conditions that trigger the formatting.

5. Preview and Apply: Excel will show you a preview of how the formatting will look. If you're satisfied, click 'OK' to apply the changes.

While Excel offers robust built-in options for conditional formatting, you can enhance your data analysis by integrating formulas into your formatting rules. This allows for highly specialized and nuanced formatting that can adapt to complex conditions, making your spreadsheets even more dynamic and insightful.

How to Create a Custom Rule with Formulas

1. Select the Range: Choose the cells you want to apply the custom rule to.

2. Navigate to the 'Home' Tab: Go to the 'Conditional Formatting' option in the 'Styles' group.

3. Choose 'New Rule': This will open a dialog box where you can define your custom rule.

4. Select 'Use a formula to determine which cells to format': This option allows you to input a custom formula.

5. Enter the Formula: In the formula field, input the Excel formula that will serve as the condition for your formatting.

6. Set the Formatting Options: Click the 'Format' button to choose the font, fill color, and other formatting options you want to apply.

7. Preview and Apply: After setting your conditions and formatting, click 'OK' to apply the rule to the selected range.

Practical Examples

Budget Management

As mentioned, you could create a rule that highlights a cell in yellow if the expenses exceed the income for that month, but only if the overage is less than $500. The formula for this could be **=AND(A2>B2, A2-B2<500),** where **A2** is the income and **B2** is the expense.

Inventory Tracking

Suppose you want to highlight items that are low in stock but have high sales. You could set a rule with a formula like **=AND(C2<10, D2>100)** where **C2** is the stock quantity and **D2** is the number of sales.

Employee Performance

If you want to highlight employees who have high sales but low customer satisfaction ratings, your formula could be **=AND(E2>1000, F2<3)** where **E2** is the sales figure and **F2** is the customer satisfaction rating.

Project Deadlines

To flag projects that are nearing their deadline but are less than 50% complete, you could use a formula like **=AND(TODAY()>G2-30, H2<0.5)** where **G2** is the project deadline and **H2** is the completion percentage.

Tips for Using Formulas in Conditional Formatting

- Relative vs. Absolute References: Be mindful of cell references in your formulas. Use relative references if you want the formula to adapt to each cell in the range.

- Debugging: If your rule isn't working as expected, double-check your formula for errors. You can test the formula in a cell first to make sure it returns the desired result.

- Order of Rules: If you have multiple conditional formatting rules, the order in which they are applied can affect the final formatting. You can manage this order in the 'Manage Rules' dialog.

Handling Large Datasets: Removing duplicates, Data Validation

As you become more proficient in Excel, you'll inevitably encounter large datasets that require specialized techniques for effective management. Two key aspects of handling such datasets are removing duplicates and implementing data validation. These techniques not only streamline your data but also enhance its integrity, making your analyses more reliable and detailed.

Removing Duplicates

Duplicate entries are more than just redundant data; they can seriously compromise the quality of your analyses. For example, if you're tracking monthly sales and duplicate entries are present, your monthly sales figures could be inflated, leading to incorrect business decisions.

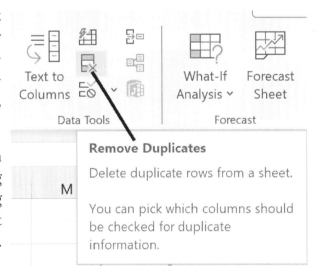

Similarly, in scientific research, duplicate data points can distort statistical analyses, rendering your results unreliable. Therefore, eliminating duplicates isn't merely an aesthetic alteration but an essential step for accurate data interpretation.

The Impact of Duplicates

- Skewed Analytics: Duplicates can inflate metrics and KPIs, leading to misleading insights.

- Wasted Resources: Duplicate records can lead to unnecessary expenditures, such as sending multiple marketing materials to the same customer.

- Data Integrity: The presence of duplicates can make it difficult to establish a single version of the truth, affecting data governance and compliance.

Step-by-Step Guide: How to Remove Duplicates

Select Your Data

1. Single Column: Click the column header to select all the data in a single column.

2. Multiple Columns: Drag your mouse across multiple column headers or hold down the 'Ctrl' key while clicking to select non-adjacent columns.

3. Specific Range: Highlight the specific range of cells you want to de-duplicate.

Navigate to the 'Data' Tab

1. Locate the Tab: The 'Data' tab is usually situated between the 'Formulas' and 'Review' tabs in the Excel ribbon.

2. Find 'Data Tools': Within the 'Data' tab, you'll find a group labeled 'Data Tools.' This is where the 'Remove Duplicates' button resides.

Choose Columns in the Dialog Box

- Column Selection: Once you click 'Remove Duplicates,' a dialog box will appear. Here, you can specify which columns to consider when identifying duplicates.

- Advanced Options: You can also choose to skip the first row if it contains headers, ensuring that your headers are not considered in the de-duplication process.

Confirm and Review

1. Execute: After making your selections, click 'OK' to initiate the process.

2. Review Results: Excel will quickly remove duplicates based on your criteria and display a message indicating how many duplicates were removed and how many unique values remain.

3. Undo Option: If you're not satisfied with the results, you can immediately press 'Ctrl + Z' to undo the action and refine your criteria.

Data Validation

Data validation is not just a feature; it's a necessity for anyone serious about maintaining the integrity of their datasets. It is like a firewall against incorrect or inconsistent data entries, ensuring your data remains reliable and actionable.

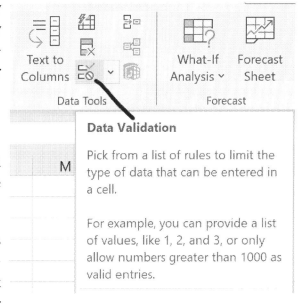

The Benefits of Data Validation

- Error Minimization: By setting predefined criteria, you significantly reduce the chance of erroneous entries.

- Data Consistency: Data validation ensures that data across different fields or spreadsheets adheres to the same format or set of values, making it easier to aggregate or analyze.

- User Guidance: Custom messages can guide users on what type of data is expected, making the data entry process more intuitive.

Types of Data Validation: A Closer Look

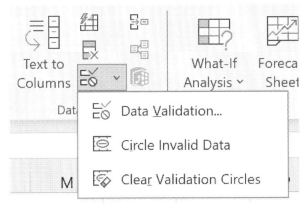

Number Ranges - You can set a minimum and/or maximum value for numerical entries. This is particularly useful in setting age restrictions or defining a permissible range for scientific measurements.

Date Ranges - Restricting date entries can be invaluable in project management to ensure deadlines fall within a project's lifecycle or in finance to ensure that fiscal entries correspond to the correct accounting period.

List of Values - Creating a dropdown list of pre-defined options not only speeds up data entry but also eliminates the possibility of spelling errors or inconsistent terminology. This is ideal for fields like 'Status' or 'Department' where the options are finite and well-defined.

Custom Rules

Excel allows you to use formulas to define your validation criteria for more complex situations. For example, you could set a rule that only allows an entry if it is both greater than 100 and a multiple of 5.

Step-by-Step: How to Implement Data Validation

Select Cells for Validation

1. Single Cell: Click on the cell where you want to apply the validation rule.

2. Multiple Cells: Drag your mouse to select a range of cells, or use 'Ctrl + Click' to select non-adjacent cells.

Navigate to the 'Data' Tab

1. Find 'Data Tools': Within the 'Data' tab, locate the 'Data Tools' group.

2. Click 'Data Validation': This will open the Data Validation dialog box.

Set Criteria and Messages

1. Choose Validation Type: In the dialog box, you'll find a 'Settings' tab where you can select the type of validation you want to apply.

2. Define Rules: Depending on the validation type, you'll be asked to enter the criteria, such as number ranges or list values.

3. Custom Messages: Switch to the 'Input Message' and 'Error Alert' tabs to set custom messages that will guide or alert the user during data entry.

Apply and Test

1. Confirm Settings: Once you're happy with your settings, click 'OK' to apply the validation.

2. Test the Validation: Try entering data into the validated cells to ensure that the rules are working as expected.

Basic Text Functions: LEFT, RIGHT, MID, CONCATENATE, TEXT

Text functions in Excel are indispensable tools for anyone who works with text data. Whether you're cleaning up imported data, preparing strings for analysis, or creating dynamic text for reports, these functions offer a range of capabilities that make your life easier.

In this section, we'll review some of the most commonly used text functions: LEFT, RIGHT, MID, CONCAT, and TEXT.

LEFT Function

The **LEFT** function is one of Excel's text functions designed to extract a specific number of characters from the beginning of a text string.

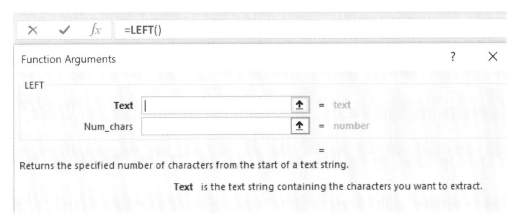

This function is particularly useful in various scenarios, such as when you need to isolate specific data from a larger dataset or when you're cleaning up imported data.

Syntax and Parameters: **=LEFT(text, [num_chars])**

- text: This is the text string from which you want to extract characters. It can be a cell reference or a text string enclosed in quotation marks.

- [num_chars]: This is an optional parameter that specifies the number of characters you want to extract. If omitted, the function will default to 1.

Practical Examples

Extracting Area Codes from Phone Numbers - If you have a column of phone numbers formatted as **(123) 456-7890** and you want to extract just the area code, you could use **=LEFT(A1, 3)** to get "123".

Isolating First Names from Full Names - If you have a list of full names in the format "John Doe" and you want to get just the first names, you can use **=LEFT(A1, FIND(" ", A1) - 1)**.

Getting File Extensions - If you have a list of file names like "document.pdf", and you want to know the first letter of the file extension, you could use **=LEFT(RIGHT(A1, 3), 1)** to get "p".

Advanced Use-Cases

- *Nested Functions*: The **LEFT** function can be nested within other functions for more complex operations. For example, **=UPPER(LEFT(A1, 2))** would extract the first two characters from cell A1 and convert them to uppercase.

- *Dynamic Extraction*: You can use other Excel functions to dynamically set the **[num_chars]** parameter. For instance, **=LEFT(A1, LEN(A1) - 4)** would extract all characters except the last four from a text string in cell A1.

RIGHT Function

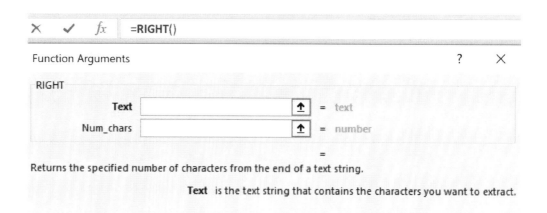

The **RIGHT** function is the counterpart to the **LEFT** function in Excel's suite of text functions. It is designed to extract a specified number of characters from the end of a text string.

This function is invaluable for various data manipulation tasks, such as isolating specific elements from strings or cleaning up data sets.

The syntax for the **RIGHT** function is simple and mirrors that of the **LEFT** function.

Advanced Use-cases

- When combined with other functions like LEN and FIND, RIGHT can be part of more complex formulas to extract text dynamically.

- Be mindful of text strings with trailing spaces, as the RIGHT function will count spaces as characters. You may need to use the TRIM function in conjunction to remove them.

MID Function

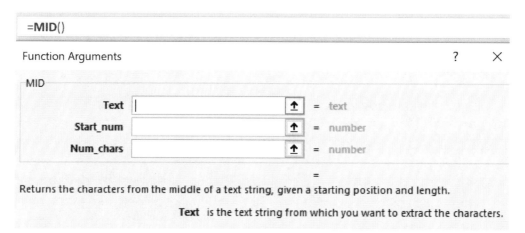

The **MID** function in Excel is a powerful tool for extracting a specific subset of characters from within a text string.

Unlike the **LEFT** and **RIGHT** functions, which are limited to extracting characters from the beginning or end of a string, **MID** gives you the flexibility to start from any position.

The syntax for the **MID** function is as follows:

=MID(text, start_num, num_chars)

- text: The text string from which you want to extract characters.
- start_num: The position of the first character you want to extract in the text string. The first character in the string is position 1.
- num_chars: The number of characters to extract, starting from start_num.

Example: If you use the formula =**MID("Excel", 2, 3)**, Excel will start at the second character ("x") and extract three characters ("xce").

CONCAT Function

Former known as CONCATENATE, the **CONCAT** function in Excel is a go-to tool for combining multiple text strings into a single string. Whether you're merging names, addresses, or any other text-based data, **CONCAT** simplifies the process.

The syntax for the CONCAT function is: =**CONCAT(text1, [text2], ...)**

- text1, text2, ...: These represent the text strings that you wish to merge. Unlike the old version of this function (CONCATENATE), CONCAT allows you to combine text across a range of cells, in addition to individual cell values.

For instance, the formula =**CONCAT("Hello ", "World")** will yield the combined string "Hello World".

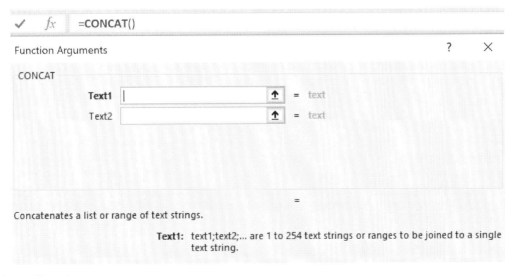

Practical Applications:

- Combining First and Last Names: **=CONCAT(A1, " ", B1)** where A1 holds the first name and B1 contains the last name.

- Creating Email Addresses: **=CONCAT(A1, "@", B1, ".com")** where A1 is the user handle and B1 is the email domain.

- Building URLs: **=CONCAT("https://", A1, "/", B1)** where A1 is the domain and B1 is the subsequent page path.

Note that CONCAT does not have a built-in delimiter feature. If you need to include delimiters (such as spaces or commas) between combined text strings, you must insert them manually between each text argument.

If you require a delimiter and also want to skip empty cells, consider using the TEXTJOIN function instead.

TEXT Function

The **TEXT** function in Excel is a powerful tool for converting numbers and dates into text while allowing you to specify the format. When you need to display data in a specific way without altering the original value, this function is there to help you.

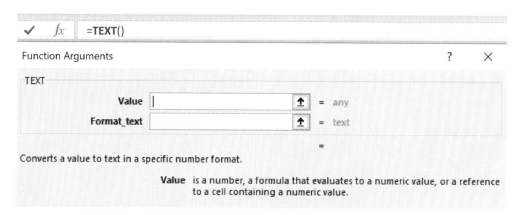

The syntax for the **TEXT** function is: **=TEXT(value, format_text)**

- value: This is the numerical or date value you want to format as text.

- format_text: This is the format code you'll use to specify how the value should be displayed as text.

For instance, the formula **=TEXT(1234.567, "$#,##0.00")** would return the string "$1,234.57".

Practical Applications

- Formatting Dates: =TEXT(A1, "dd-mmm-yyyy") where A1 contains a date, will format it as "01-Jan-2023".

- Percentage Formatting: =TEXT(B1, "0%") where B1 contains a decimal like 0.25, will format it as "25%".

- Phone Numbers: =TEXT(C1, "(###) ###-####") where C1 contains a number like 1234567890, will format it as "(123) 456-7890".

Advanced Usage

You can also combine the **TEXT** function with other functions for more complex formatting. For instance, if you want to create a full date string: **=CONCAT("The date is ", TEXT(TODAY(), "dd-mmm-yyyy"))**

This will return a string like "The date is 01-Jan-2023".

Practical Applications of Text Functions

Data Cleaning

The **LEFT**, **RIGHT**, and **MID** functions are indispensable for cleaning up messy data. Imagine you need to import a dataset where phone numbers are in the format "(123) 456-7890". In such a case, these functions can be employed to extract only the numerical components.

- *Example*: **=MID(A1, 2, 3) & MID(A1, 7, 3) & RIGHT(A1, 4)** where A1 contains "(123) 456-7890" would return "1234567890".

Dynamic Reporting

The **CONCAT** function can be used to create dynamic text in reports. This is especially useful for dashboards where you want to display text based on data in other cells.

- *Example*: **=CONCAT("Sales for Q1: $", TEXT(B1, "#,##0"))** where B1 contains the sales figure for Q1.

Data Formatting

The **TEXT** function is an excellent tool for ensuring that numerical data adheres to specific text formatting rules. This makes your data easier to read and analyze, especially in reports or presentations.

- *Example*: **=TEXT(C1, "$#,##0.00")** where C1 contains a financial figure, will format it as currency.

Step-by-Step: How to Use Text Functions

1. Select a Cell: Choose the cell where you want the function result to appear.

2. Enter the Function: Type the function you want to use, followed by an opening parenthe-

sis. For example, type =LEFT(to start using the LEFT function.

3. Input Arguments: Enter the required arguments for the function. For instance, if you're using the LEFT function, you would enter the text string and the number of characters you want to extract.

4. Close and Execute: Close the parenthesis and press 'Enter'. Excel will execute the function and display the result in the selected cell.

Date and Time Functions

Excel's date and time functions are essential tools for anyone who needs to manage schedules, perform time-based calculations, or keep track of important dates. These functions allow you to extract, manipulate, and perform calculations with date and time data in a variety of formats.

Key Functions

TODAY and NOW

TODAY: Returns the current date.

- Syntax: **=TODAY()**

- Example: **=TODAY()** would return the current date.

NOW: Returns the current date and time.

- Syntax: **=NOW()**

- Example: **=NOW()** would return the current date and time.

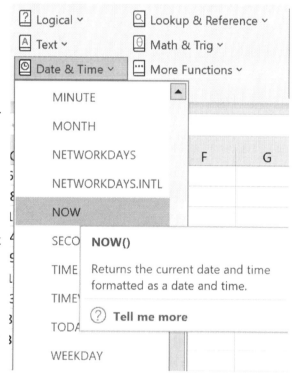

DATE and TIME

- **DATE**: Creates a date based on individual year, month, and day components.

    ○ Syntax: **=DATE(year, month, day)**

    ○ Example: **=DATE(2023, 10, 6)** would return October 6, 2023.

- **TIME**: Creates a time based on individual hour, minute, and second components.

    ○ Syntax: **=TIME(hour, minute, second)**

    ○ Example: **=TIME(12, 30, 0)** would return 12:30:00.

DATEDIF and NETWORKDAYS

- **DATEDIF**: Calculates the difference between two dates.
    - Syntax: =**DATEDIF(start_date, end_date, "unit")**
    - Example: =**DATEDIF(A1, B1, "D")** would return the number of days between the dates in cells A1 and B1.
- **NETWORKDAYS**: Calculates the number of whole workdays between two dates.
    - Syntax: =**NETWORKDAYS(start_date, end_date, [holidays])**
    - Example: =**NETWORKDAYS(A1, B1)** would return the number of workdays between the dates in cells A1 and B1, excluding weekends and holidays.

Practical Applications

- *Project Management*: Use **DATEDIF** and **NETWORKDAYS** to calculate project timelines and deadlines.
- *Financial Analysis*: Use **TODAY** and **NOW** for real-time data tracking and reporting.
- *Event Planning*: Use **DATE** and **TIME** to schedule events and set reminders.

Step-by-Step: How to Use Date and Time Functions

1. Select a Cell: Choose the cell where you want the function result to appear.
2. Enter the Function: Type the function you want to use, followed by an opening parenthesis.
3. Input Arguments: Enter the required arguments for the function.
4. Close and Execute: Close the parenthesis and press 'Enter'.

By becoming proficient in these date and time functions, you'll infuse an extra layer of finesse into your Excel skills. This will empower you to tackle a wider variety of tasks with precision and efficiency.

Chapter Four

DAY 4: DATA VISUALIZATION

Welcome to the fourth day of our journey through Excel. Today, we're going to explore a realm that brings your data to life in the most vivid ways possible—data visualization. Up until now, we've been laying the groundwork by focusing on data management, calculations, and text functions. While these are all critical skills, they often serve as the behind-the-scenes work. Data visualization, on the other hand, is your moment on stage. It's where you get to present your data in a way that makes people sit up and take notice.

Imagine you're a business analyst. You've crunched the numbers, and you know your company had an excellent quarter. But how do you convey that to your team or stakeholders? A table full of numbers is accurate but hardly inspiring. This is where data visualization takes the stage. With the appropriate chart or graph, you can not only demonstrate a successful quarter for the company but also emphasize trends, showcase key accomplishments, and build a persuasive argument for future strategies.

But it's not just about making things look good. The type of chart you choose, how you format it, and even the colors you pick can profoundly impact how well your audience understands the information you're presenting. That's why today, you will learn everything from the basics of creating charts and graphs to the nuances of selecting the right format and customizing it to tell the most compelling story.

I'll also introduce you to Sparklines, a feature that allows you to include mini-charts within individual cells for quick insights. As a final touch, we'll discuss some best practices to ensure that your data visualization efforts are not only practical but also ethical.

Let's get started on making your data visually eloquent.

Creating Charts and Graphs

The first step in your data visualization journey is learning how to create charts and graphs. These visual elements form the foundation for presenting your data in a clear and impactful manner. But before getting into the mechanics, let's discover why charts and graphs are indispensable for transforming raw data into meaningful insights.

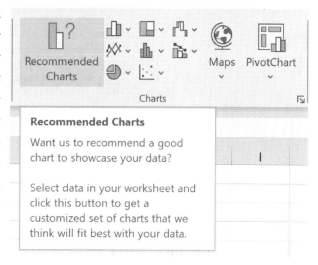

Now, consider this example: You're sitting in a meeting, and someone hands you a spreadsheet filled with rows and columns of numbers. Your eyes glaze over as you try to make sense of it all. Now, picture the same data presented as a bar chart or a line graph. Suddenly, the trends become clear, the outliers stand out, and the story behind the numbers comes to life. That's the power of charts and graphs—they transform abstract data into concrete understanding.

How to Create a Basic Chart

Creating a basic chart in Excel is not just about clicking a few buttons; it's about making informed choices at each step to ensure your chart effectively communicates the data's story. Let's take a closer look at each step in the process.

Select Your Data - The first and most crucial step is selecting the data you want to visualize. Make sure that you highlight not just the numerical data but also the corresponding row and column headers. This will make it easier for Excel to understand what each data point represents, which, in turn, makes the subsequent steps smoother.

Go to the 'Insert' Tab - Once your data is selected, go to the 'Insert' tab located in the Ribbon at the top of your Excel window. This tab is a treasure trove of visualization tools. You'll find options for Column charts, Line charts, Pie charts, and many more specialized chart types. Each chart type serves a different purpose and is suited for different kinds of data, so choose wisely.

Choose Your Chart Type - After navigating to the 'Insert' tab, you'll need to decide on the type of chart that best represents your data. If you're unsure, hover your mouse over each chart type. Excel will provide a brief description of what each chart is best used for. Once you've made your choice, click on it, and Excel will generate a basic chart based on your selected data.

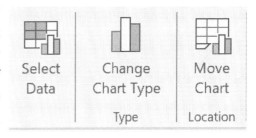

Adjust the Axis and Labels - Your chart is now visible, but it's far from complete. The next step is to adjust the axis labels and other textual elements to make your chart as informative as possible. To do this, click on the chart to activate the 'Chart Tools' tabs in the Ribbon. Here, you can modify the chart title, axis titles, and data labels. You can also add additional elements like trend lines or error bars.

Preview and Edit - Finally, take a step back and preview your chart. Ask yourself if it accurately represents the data and conveys your intended message. If something seems off, don't hesitate to go back and make adjustments. Excel makes it easy to edit charts even after they've been created. You can change the chart type, update the data range, or tweak the visual elements until you're satisfied.

Chart Elements

Each element used to make up a chart serves a specific function and contributes to the chart's overall readability and impact.

The title is more than just a label; it's the headline of your data story. A well-crafted title immediately informs the viewer what the chart is about and sets the context for the data being presented. It should be concise yet descriptive enough to give a clear idea of the chart's purpose. For example, instead of a generic title like "Sales Data," a more informative title would be "Monthly Sales Data for Q1 2023."

Axis labels are the signposts that guide the viewer through the data landscape. The X-axis typically represents the independent variable, such as time or categories, while the Y-axis represents the dependent variable, like sales figures or percentages. Properly labeled axes remove any ambiguity about what the data points signify. For instance, specifying that the Y-axis represents "Revenue in USD" is more informative than just "Revenue."

The **data series** is the actual data you're plotting, represented through bars in a bar chart, lines in a line chart, or slices in a pie chart, among other shapes. The way you choose to display this data will depend on the type of chart you're using and the nature of your data. For example, a line chart is excellent for showing trends over time, while a bar chart might be better for comparing individual categories.

The **legend** is a decoder ring for your chart, explaining what different colors, shapes, or lines represent. This is especially important in charts with multiple data series. A well-placed and easy-to-read legend helps the viewer understand the chart without having to refer back to the text for explanations.

Gridlines may seem like a minor detail, but they play a significant role in making your chart easy to read. By providing reference lines that viewers can use to gauge values, gridlines enhance the chart's readability. They are particularly useful in complex charts with large datasets, where pinpointing exact values can be challenging.

Choosing the Right Chart Type for Your Data

The art of data visualization is not just about creating a chart but also about selecting the right kind of chart for your data. The type of chart you choose can make a significant difference in how well your audience understands the information you're presenting.

Column and Bar Charts

Opt for column charts when you want to show trends over time, such as monthly sales figures. Bar charts are excellent for comparing quantities across different categories, like sales by product type.

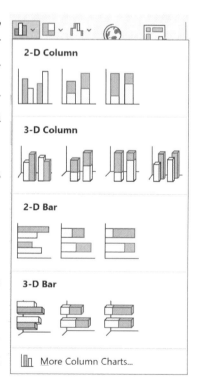

- Tip: If you're dealing with multiple data series, consider using a stacked column or bar chart to show the composition of each category.

- Common Mistake: Avoid using too many bars or columns, as it can make the chart cluttered and hard to read.

Line Charts

Line charts are your go-to for showing trends over a continuous period, especially when you have many data points.

- Tip: Use markers for each data point on the line to make individual values easier to read. Also, consider using different line styles (dotted, dashed) if you're plotting multiple series.

- Common Mistake: Don't use line charts for categorical data; they imply a continuous relationship that may not exist.

Pie Charts

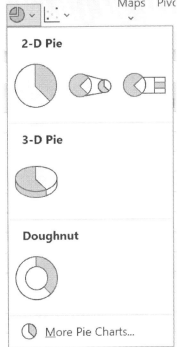

Pie charts are effective for showing the relative proportions of different categories that make up a whole, such as market share by company.

Tip: Limit the number of slices to 5-7 for better readability. Use labels or a legend to identify each slice clearly.

Common Mistake: Avoid using pie charts for comparing individual values or for showing trends over time. Also, be cautious about using 3D pie charts, as they can distort proportions.

Scatter Plots

Scatter plots are ideal for showing the relationship between two numerical variables. They excel in revealing correlations, trends, or outliers.

Tip: Add a trendline to your scatter plot to make it easier to interpret the relationship between variables. You can also use color to represent a third variable, adding another layer of information.

- Common Mistake: Avoid using scatter plots for categorical data or when you have less than 10 data points, as it may not provide meaningful insights.

Area Charts

Area charts effectively show the volume or magnitude of a trend over time. When you aim to highlight the cumulative impact of a data series, you can use them.

- Tip: If you're using multiple data series, consider using a stacked area chart to show the relationship between individual series and the whole.

- Common Mistake: Be cautious when using area charts with multiple overlapping series, as it can make the chart hard to interpret.

Specialized Charts

Radar charts are great for comparing multiple variables for different categories or entities. Heatmaps help show the density or intensity of variables in a two-dimensional space.

- Tip: Use color gradients effectively in heatmaps to represent the range of values. In radar charts, make sure to label each axis clearly for better readability.

- Common Mistake: These specialized charts can be complex; use them only when simpler charts like bar or line charts won't suffice.

Custom Charts

Custom charts are your go-to option when you have specific or complex data visualization needs that standard chart types can't meet.

- Tip: Experiment with combining different chart types, like a line chart overlaying a column chart, to provide multiple perspectives on the data.

- Common Mistake: While customization offers flexibility, avoid making the chart too complicated, as it can confuse rather than clarify.

Customizing and Formatting Your Charts

Creating a chart is just the beginning; the real magic lies in customizing and formatting it to tell a compelling story. Excel offers a plethora of options to tailor your charts to your specific needs. Here's a step-by-step guide to help you master the art of chart customization.

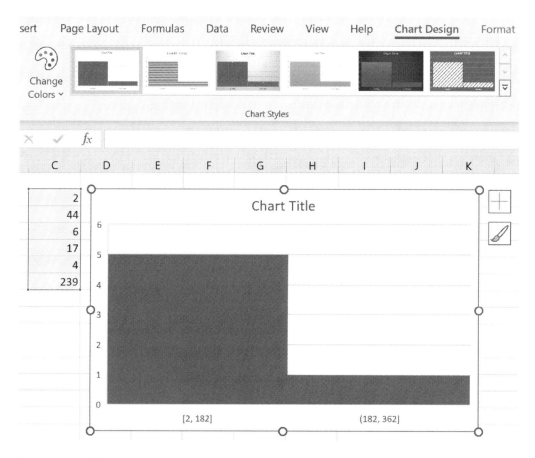

Step 1: Select Your Chart

The first step in the customization process is to select the chart you wish to modify. Simply click anywhere within the chart area. You'll know the chart is selected when small squares, commonly referred to as "handles," appear around its perimeter. These handles can also be used to resize the chart, offering another layer of customization right from the get-go.

Step 2: Access the Design and Format Tabs

Upon selecting your chart, you'll notice that two new tabs appear in the Excel ribbon at the top of your screen: the 'Design' and 'Format' tabs. These are not just tabs; think of them as your control centers for chart customization. They contain a wide array of tools and options that allow you to tweak nearly every aspect of your chart.

Step 3: Add or Remove Chart Elements

Navigating the Design Tab - The 'Design' tab is where you'll find options to add or remove various chart elements. Look for the 'Add Chart Element' button; it's your gateway to adding titles, axis labels, gridlines, and more.

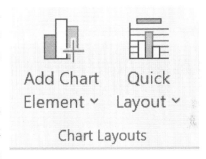

Adding a Chart Title - For instance, if you want to add a title to your chart, you would go to 'Add Chart Element,' hover over 'Chart Title' in the dropdown menu, and then you'll see options for where you want the title to be placed. You can choose to have it above the chart, centered, overlaying the chart, or even more specific positions.

Let's say you're working on a sales report, and you want to add a title that says "Monthly Sales Data." Here's how you'd do it:

1. Click on 'Add Chart Element.'

2. Hover over 'Chart Title.'

3. Choose 'Above Chart.'

4. A text box will appear above your chart saying "Chart Title." Click on it.

5. Type "Monthly Sales Data."

And just like that, your chart now has a title that clearly indicates what it represents, making it easier for your audience to understand the data you're presenting.

Step 4: Customize Chart Styles

Navigating the Design Tab Again - The 'Design' tab isn't just for adding or removing elements; it's also where you can change the overall style of your chart. Two key features here are 'Change Chart Type' and 'Chart Styles.'

Changing to a 3D Style - For example, if you want to give your chart a more dynamic look by changing it to a 3D style, you can easily do so. Navigate to 'Change Chart Type', and a dialog box will appear with various chart types. Scroll down until you find the 3D options, and select the one that best suits your data.

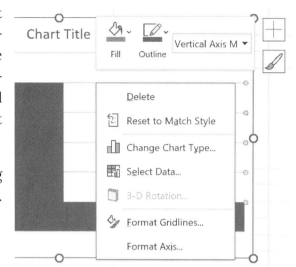

Consider this: You have a column chart showing quarterly revenue, and you want to make it 3D. Here's how you do it:

1. Click on 'Change Chart Type.'

2. Scroll to find the 3D Column options.

3. Select the 3D style you prefer.

4. Click 'OK.'

Your column chart will transform into a 3D chart, adding a layer of depth and visual interest.

Step 5: Modify Data Series and Axes

Switch over to the 'Format' tab to get into the nitty-gritty details of your chart. Here, you can change the color, size, and style of your data series and axes.

Changing Bar Color - For instance, to change the color of a bar in a bar chart, you would right-click on the bar itself, then choose 'Format Data Series.' A sidebar will appear on the right. Navigate to 'Fill & Line,' which looks like a paint bucket, and select your desired color.

Step 6: Add Data Labels and Annotations

Data labels can be incredibly useful for providing context to your charts. To add them, head back to the 'Design' tab and click on 'Add Chart Element,' then hover over 'Data Labels.'

Adding Labels to a Pie Chart - For example, if you have a pie chart and you want to display the exact percentage each slice represents, do the following:

1. Select the pie chart.

2. Go to 'Add Chart Element.'

3. Hover over 'Data Labels.'

4. Choose where you want the labels to appear—inside or outside the pie slices.

Your pie chart will now display the exact percentages, making it easier for your audience to understand the data at a glance.

Step 7: Fine-Tune with Advanced Formatting

Sometimes, the options available in the 'Design' and 'Format' tabs aren't enough for your specific needs. That's where right-clicking comes in handy. Right-clicking on various elements of the chart will open a context menu with more advanced options.

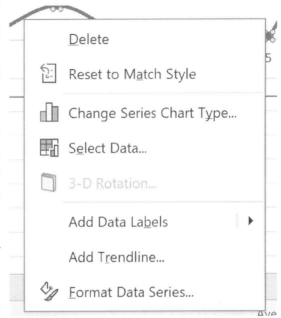

Adding a Trendline to a Scatter Plot - For example, if you have a scatter plot and you want to add a trendline to better understand the relationship between your variables, you can do so with a simple right-click.

1. Right-click on one of the data points in your scatter plot.
2. From the context menu, select 'Add Trendline.'

Your scatter plot will now include a trendline, helping you and your audience to see the general trend of the data at a glance.

Step 8: Preview and Edit

Always take a moment to preview your chart after making changes. This ensures that everything looks as you intended and allows you to catch any errors or inconsistencies.

Quick Edits - If something doesn't look right, don't worry. You can easily undo your last action by pressing Ctrl+Z or clicking the 'Undo' button in the toolbar. This allows for quick edits without having to start over.

Step 9: Save Your Customized Chart as a Template

Once you've customized a chart to your liking, you might want to use the same style for future charts. Excel allows you to save your customized chart as a template, making it easy to apply the same look and feel to new charts.

How to Save

1. Right-click on the chart area.
2. From the context menu, choose 'Save as Template.'

For instance, if you've created a highly customized column chart for your monthly sales report, you can save it as a template named 'Monthly Sales Report.' The next time you need to create a similar chart, you can start with your template, saving you time and giving consistency to your reports.

Introduction to Sparklines

Sparklines are essentially mini-charts that fit into a single cell, providing a visual representation of data without needing a full-blown chart. Developed by data visualization expert Edward Tufte, sparklines offer a way to present trends and variations in a compact, simple, and intuitive manner. They can be used for dashboards and reports where space is at a premium, and you want to offer a quick snapshot of data trends.

Why use sparklines? Sparklines are simple and efficient. They let you quickly see the overall trend of a data series at a glance, making it easy to understand without delving into details. Whether you're tracking sales, website traffic, or stock prices, sparklines provide immediate insights. They are perfect for fast comparisons used in business analytics, financial reports, and data summaries.

Types of Sparklines

Excel offers three main types of sparklines:

Line Sparklines: Ideal for displaying trends over a period, such as monthly sales or temperature variations.

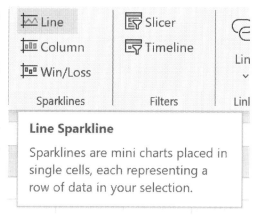

- Visual Elements: A simple line graph that rises and falls according to the data points.

- Example: If you have monthly revenue data for a year, a line sparkline will show you the ups and downs at a glance.

Column Sparklines: Excellent for showing the magnitude of variations in your data points, like test scores or inventory levels.

- Visual Elements: Vertical bars represent each data point, allowing for easy comparison.

- Example: If you're tracking the number of customer complaints received each day of the week, a column sparkline would visually represent this data in a compact form.

Win/Loss Sparklines: These are particularly useful for showing a series of positive and negative values, often used in financial contexts like trading.

- Visual Elements: Displays simple bars going up for wins (positive values) and down for losses (negative values).
- Example: If you're analyzing a stock's daily performance, a Win/Loss sparkline could quickly show you the days the stock gained or lost value.

How to Create Sparklines in Excel

An example of what the different types of sparklines look like

1. *Select the Data*: First, highlight the range of cells containing the data you want to visualize. Make sure the data is organized to suit the type of sparkline you want to use.

2. *Navigate to the 'Insert' Tab*: Once your data is selected, go to the 'Insert' tab on the Excel ribbon. Here, you'll find the 'Sparklines' group, which is your starting point for creating these mini-charts.

3. *Choose the Type*: Click on the type of sparkline you wish to create. You'll have options for Line, Column, or Win/Loss. The choice should align with what you want to visualize. For example, if you're interested in trends, go for Line Sparklines.

4. *Specify the Location*: After selecting the type, a dialog box will appear, asking you to specify the cell where you want the sparkline to appear. This is usually a cell adjacent to the data you're visualizing, but it can be anywhere in the worksheet. Once you've chosen the cell, click 'OK.'

5. *Review and Adjust*: Your sparkline will now appear in the specified cell. Take a moment to review it. If it's not quite right, you can easily adjust its type or formatting by selecting it and revisiting the 'Sparklines' group in the 'Insert' tab.

Customizing Sparklines

Change Color: To make your sparklines blend seamlessly with the rest of your report, you can change their color. Simply select the sparkline, go to the 'Design' tab under 'Sparkline Tools', and choose a new color from the 'Sparkline Color' option.

Add Markers: For line sparklines, adding markers can provide additional context. Markers for the high point, low point, first point, and last point can be added. Navigate to the 'Design' tab and check the boxes for the markers you wish to include under 'Show'.

Adjust Scale: If you're comparing multiple sparklines, having a consistent scale can make interpretation easier. To manually adjust the scale, go to the 'Axis' option under the 'Design' tab. Here, you can set a 'Custom Value' for both the minimum and maximum axis values.

Practical Applications

I can't emphasize enough the utility of sparklines in sales dashboards. These concise data visualizations provide managers with a quick method to assess sales trends. Whether it's comparing quarterly product performance or evaluating the effectiveness of sales teams, sparklines prove to be a valuable tool for fast and meaningful analysis.

Moving on to performance reports, sparklines prove equally helpful. They offer a streamlined way to monitor key performance indicators (KPIs) over a given time frame. This is particularly beneficial when you're juggling multiple metrics, such as website traffic, customer satisfaction scores, or even employee performance. A quick look at a sparkline can instantly tell you whether you're meeting your targets or if there's a need for intervention.

In financial analysis, sparklines, especially the Win/Loss type, have distinct advantages. Investors and financial analysts frequently need to make speedy, well-informed decisions. A Win/Loss sparkline can quickly show the months when an asset was profitable or not, helping in swift decision-making.

Limitations and Best Practices

- *High-Level Overview*: Sparklines are designed to provide a high-level, quick look at data trends. They are not meant to replace detailed charts but rather to complement them.

- *Visibility*: Because of their compact size, sparklines can sometimes be overlooked. Make sure to place them where they can effectively support the data story you are telling.

- *Complementary Use*: Sparklines are most effective when used in conjunction with other, more detailed forms of data visualization. For example, a dashboard might include both detailed charts and sparklines to provide both depth and breadth in data analysis.

Visualizing Different Types of Data

Data visualization is a powerful tool that can transform raw data into meaningful insights. However, the effectiveness of this tool depends on the type of data you're working with and how you choose to visualize it. In this section, you'll discover specific tips for visualizing three types of data: time-series data, geographic data, and statistical distributions.

Time-Series Data

Time-series data is a sequence of data points collected or recorded at specific time intervals. This type of data is ubiquitous in various fields, from tracking a company's quarterly sales and monitoring website traffic over a month to observing temperature changes in a city over a week. The key characteristic of time-series data is its temporal order, making it crucial to use the right visualization techniques to capture trends, patterns, and anomalies effectively.

Line Charts

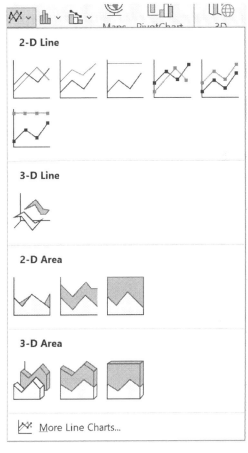

Line charts are the preferred visualization method for time-series data for a reason. They excel at showing trends over a period, making it easier to identify increases, decreases, or patterns. The x-axis typically represents time, while the y-axis represents the variable you are measuring.

Advanced Tips:

- Markers: Adding markers to each data point can make it easier to read individual values.

- Line Styles: If you're plotting multiple series on the same chart, using different line styles like dotted or dashed lines can help differentiate between them.

Common Mistakes:

- Categorical Data: Line charts are NOT suitable for categorical data, as they imply a continuous relationship between points that may not exist.

- Axis Scaling: Be cautious with the scaling of your y-axis. An inappropriate scale can either exaggerate or minimize the appearance of trends.

Area Charts

Area charts are an extension of line charts by filling the area between the line and the x-axis with color. This visual element can emphasize the volume or magnitude of changes over time, making the data more impactful.

Advanced Tips:

- Stacked Area Charts: If you're dealing with multiple data series, a stacked area chart can be incredibly useful. It shows the relationship between individual series and the cumulative total, making it easier to understand the distribution of each component over time.

Common Mistakes:

- Overlapping Series: When using multiple series in an area chart, the overlapping colors can make the chart confusing and hard to interpret. Transparency settings can sometimes alleviate this issue, but it's generally best to avoid too much overlap.

- Inappropriate Use: Like line charts, area charts are not suitable for categorical data. They are best used when you want to show how a quantity changes over time.

Geographic Data

Geographic data involves measurements or observations that are tied to specific geographical locations. This type of data is crucial in various applications, from public policy and urban planning to marketing and environmental studies. Visualizing geographic data correctly is essential for understanding spatial relationships and making informed decisions.

Maps

Maps offer an intuitive way to visualize geographic data. They provide the spatial context that helps viewers easily identify patterns, trends, and correlations across different regions or locations.

Advanced Tips:

- Color Gradients: Utilizing color gradients can effectively represent a range of values. Darker shades usually signify higher values, while lighter shades indicate lower values.

- Interactive Features: Modern data visualization tools allow for interactive maps where additional data can be displayed through hover or click actions. This interactivity can make your map not just a static image but a dynamic source of information.

Common Mistakes:

- Color Overload: Using too many colors can make the map confusing and challenging to interpret. Stick to a simple color scheme that can effectively convey the data.

- Geographic Accuracy: Always ensure that the geographic boundaries used in your map are accurate. Inaccurate or outdated boundaries can lead to misinterpretation and could compromise the integrity of your data.

Bubble Maps

Bubble maps are an extension of traditional maps, where bubbles or circles are used to represent data values at specific geographic locations. This adds an extra layer of information, making the data visualization richer and more nuanced.

Advanced Tips:

- Scale Consistency: It's crucial to use a consistent scale for the size of the bubbles. This ensures that the viewer can accurately interpret the data.
- Labels and Legends: Adding labels or legends can provide context for the bubble sizes, making the map more informative and easier to understand.

Common Mistakes:

- Overcrowding: Placing too many bubbles on the map can lead to overcrowding, making it difficult to distinguish between individual data points.
- Proportional Representation: Ensure that the size of each bubble is proportional to the data value it represents. Inconsistent sizing can lead to misleading visuals and incorrect interpretations.

Statistical Distributions

Statistical distributions are a key aspect of data analysis and statistics. They let us grasp how data is spread across different categories or intervals. This concept has various applications, from understanding a company's sales across its product range to analyzing survey responses or studying the age distribution within a population.

Bar Charts

Bar charts are incredibly versatile and help compare quantities across different categories. They are straightforward to read and interpret, making them one of the most commonly used types of data visualization.

Advanced Tips:

- Stacked Bar Charts: If you're dealing with multiple data series, a stacked bar chart can show not only the total size of each category but also its composition, adding depth to your analysis.

Common Mistakes:

- Overcluttering: While it might be tempting to include as much information as possible, too many bars can make the chart cluttered and challenging to interpret. Stick to the most relevant categories for your analysis.

Histograms

Unlike bar charts, histograms are used for visualizing the distribution of continuous data. They divide the data into intervals, known as "bins," and display the frequency of data points within each bin.

Advanced Tips:

- Bin Selection: The choice of bin size can significantly impact the histogram's appearance and interpretability. Too many bins can make it look like a line chart, while too few can oversimplify the data.

Common Mistakes:

- Categorical Data: Histograms are not suitable for categorical data. Using them in such a context can lead to misinterpretation.

Box Plots

Box plots provide a more comprehensive view of data distribution. They are based on a five-number summary: the minimum, first quartile, median, third quartile, and maximum. They also identify outliers in the data set.

Advanced Tips:

- Comparative Analysis: Box plots are particularly useful when comparing distributions across different categories or groups. They can provide insights into the variability and central tendency of each group.

Common Mistakes:

- Time-Series Data: Box plots are not well-suited for time-series data as they don't capture trends over time.

Data Visualization Best Practices

While Excel offers a myriad of tools for creating charts, graphs, and other visual aids, the effectiveness of these tools hinges on your ability to use them wisely. Here are some best practices to elevate your data visualization game in Excel.

Understand Your Audience

Before venturing into data visualization, it's imperative to have a clear understanding of your audience's background and needs. Are you presenting to industry experts who are well-versed in the subject matter or to a general audience that may require more explanation? The level of complexity in your visualizations should be directly influenced by your audience's familiarity with the topic. Tailoring your charts and graphs to the audience's expertise ensures your message is accessible and meaningful.

Choose the Right Chart Type

Selecting the appropriate chart type is a pivotal step in effective data visualization. As previously mentioned, Excel offers a variety of options, each designed to showcase different kinds of data. For instance, column and bar charts excel at comparing individual items across categories, line charts are particularly effective for illustrating trends over time, and pie charts are optimal for representing proportions. The key is to choose a chart type that aligns with the narrative you want your data to convey, thereby making your visualization as impactful as possible.

Keep It Simple

The allure of intricate graphics and vibrant colors can be strong, but when it comes to data visualization, less is often more. Overcomplicating a chart with unnecessary design elements can muddle the message and distract from the data itself. Aim for a minimalist design that allows the data to take center stage. By focusing on clarity and simplicity, you make it easier for the audience to grasp the key points without getting lost in visual clutter.

Use Consistent Scales and Units

Maintaining uniform scales and units is crucial for an accurate and honest representation of your data. Mixing different units or scales can create a misleading impression, skewing the audience's understanding of the information presented. Always ensure that you're using consistent units and scales, especially when comparing multiple data sets. Additionally, clearly label your axes to provide context and eliminate any potential for confusion. This consistency reinforces the integrity of your data visualization, making it easier to interpret.

1. *Highlight Key Data Points*

When you're dealing with a complex dataset, it's essential to guide your audience's focus towards the most important information. Utilize visual cues like contrasting colors, bold labels, or special markers to emphasize key data points or significant trends. By making these elements stand out, you not only capture attention but also facilitate a deeper understanding of the data's primary messages.

2. Provide Context

Data in isolation can be ambiguous or misleading; it gains meaning through context. To ensure your audience fully grasps the implications of your data, supplement your visualizations with informative titles, legends, and annotations. These elements can clarify what the axes represent, explain any abbreviations or symbols used, and provide further information that may not be immediately obvious from the data alone. Providing context enriches the narrative around your data, making it more comprehensive and relatable.

3. Test and Revise

Creating a data visualization is rarely a one-and-done process. After your initial draft, you need to seek feedback from a diverse set of viewers, including colleagues, experts in the field, or members of your target audience. Listen to their impressions and critiques, and be prepared to make revisions. This iterative process helps refine your visualization, enhancing its clarity, accuracy, and overall impact.

4. Keep Accessibility in Mind

Data visualization should be inclusive, catering to a wide range of viewers, including those with visual impairments or color vision deficiencies. To make your charts and graphs more accessible, consider using patterns or textures in addition to colors to differentiate between data points or categories. Also, explore Excel's accessibility features, like alt text for charts, to ensure that your visualizations can be understood by as many people as possible.

5. Verify Your Data

Before you finalize and present your data visualization, it's imperative to double-check the accuracy of your data. Even the most visually stunning chart loses all credibility if it's based on flawed or incorrect data. Ensure that your data sources are reliable, that you've performed any necessary data cleaning, and that all calculations are correct. A meticulously verified dataset enhances your visualization's trustworthiness and safeguards against the potential repercussions of disseminating misleading information.

By adhering to these best practices, you'll be well on your way to creating impactful and effective data visualizations in Excel. These guidelines are designed to enhance the accuracy and impact of your visual representations, whether you're crafting a team report, sharing insights with stakeholders, or conducting personal data analysis.

Chapter Five

DAY 5: INTERMEDIATE FUNCTIONS AND FEATURES

Welcome to Day 5, where we kick your Excel skills up a notch from basic to intermediate. Today, we will discuss Excel's advanced features, enhancing your data handling, analysis, and presentation skills.

We'll begin by demystifying Lookup Functions like VLOOKUP, HLOOKUP, and the powerful INDEX/MATCH combo, which can be your best allies in navigating large datasets. Then, we'll transition into the transformative world of Pivot Tables, a feature that turns raw data into meaningful reports with just a few clicks.

You will also learn advanced conditional formatting techniques to visualize data in ways you've never imagined. Array Formulas and Functions will be our next stop, offering you the tools to perform complex calculations like a breeze. Finally, we'll explore how to link, embed, and import data, connecting Excel to the world beyond its gridlines.

Introduction to Lookup Functions: VLOOKUP, HLOOKUP, INDEX/MATCH

In today's first segment, you will get familiar with the world of Lookup Functions, specifically focusing on VLOOKUP, HLOOKUP, and the INDEX/MATCH combination. These functions quietly empower Excel, allowing you to navigate extensive datasets, locate desired information, and link data across multiple tables.

VLOOKUP

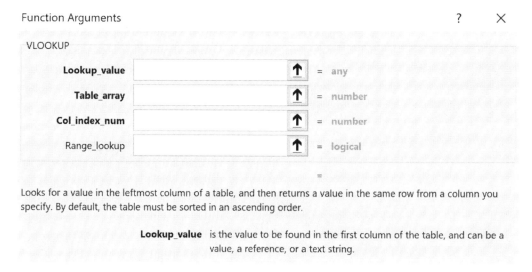

The VLOOKUP function consists of four arguments:

1. **lookup_value**: This is the value you want to search for in the first column of your table array.

2. **table_array**: This is the range of cells that contains the data you want to search through.

3. **col_index_num**: This is the column index number of the value to be returned. The first column in the table_array is 1, the second column is 2, and so on.

4. **range_lookup**: This is an optional argument. If TRUE, VLOOKUP will look for an approximate match. If FALSE, it will look for an exact match.

VLOOKUP is incredibly versatile and can be used in various scenarios:

- Inventory Management: If you have a list of product IDs and their corresponding stock levels, you can quickly find out how much stock you have for a particular product.

- Customer Information: For a dataset containing customer IDs and their details, VLOOKUP can swiftly provide you with specific customer information.
- Grade Lookup: In an educational setting, you can use VLOOKUP to find students' grades based on their roll numbers.

While VLOOKUP is powerful, it has some limitations:

- Left-to-Right Lookup Only: VLOOKUP can only look for values to the right of the lookup_value. It cannot return values to the left.
- First Match Only: If there are multiple instances of the lookup_value, VLOOKUP will return the first match it finds.

To overcome these limitations, you can use INDEX/MATCH or consider using the newer XLOOKUP function if you're using a more recent version of Excel.

Here are some advanced tips:

- **Nested VLOOKUP**: You can nest VLOOKUP within other functions to perform more complex tasks.
- **Dynamic Column Index**: Instead of hardcoding the column index number, you can use other functions like MATCH to make it dynamic.

Let's revisit our employee salary example. Suppose you also have a column for department names, and you want to find out not just the salary but also the department of a specific employee. You could use a nested VLOOKUP function like this:

=VLOOKUP("EMP123", A2:C10, MATCH("Department", A1:C1, 0), FALSE)

This will search for the employee ID "EMP123" in the range A2:C10 and return the department name, dynamically finding the correct column using MATCH.

HLOOKUP

HLOOKUP, short for Horizontal Lookup, is the row-wise counterpart to VLOOKUP. While VLOOKUP is tailored for vertical data layouts, HLOOKUP is designed for horizontal layouts. The function searches for a value in the first row of a table range and returns a value in the same column from another row.

The syntax for HLOOKUP is quite similar to that of VLOOKUP, with the main difference being the orientation of the data:

=HLOOKUP(lookup_value, table_array, row_index_num, [range_lookup])

Here, **row_index_num** specifies the row number in the table_array from which to retrieve a value. The first row is 1, the second row is 2, and so on.

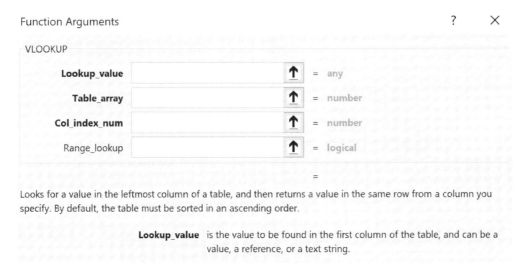

Example in Context – In a dataset where the first row contains the months of the year, and the rows below contain sales figures, you could use HLOOKUP to find the sales for a specific month:

=**HLOOKUP("March", A1:G3, 2, FALSE)**

This formula would search for "March" in the first row and return the sales figure from the second row in the same column where "March" was found.

HLOOKUP is particularly useful in scenarios where:

- Financial Statements: If you have a balance sheet where account titles are in the first row, and monthly figures follow, HLOOKUP can quickly pull data for a specific month.

- Event Scheduling: In a schedule where days or dates are listed horizontally, HLOOKUP can find details for a specific day.

Just like VLOOKUP, HLOOKUP also has its limitations, such as only being able to search from left to right and returning the first match it finds. For more advanced capabilities, you might refer back to the INDEX/MATCH combination mentioned in the VLOOKUP section.

While HLOOKUP is less commonly used than VLOOKUP, it can be combined with other Excel functions for more complex queries. For example, you could use a nested HLOOKUP within an IF function to return customized results.

INDEX/MATCH

The INDEX/MATCH combination is often considered the more flexible alternative to VLOOKUP and HLOOKUP. This dynamic duo can handle both vertical and horizontal lookups and is not affected by column or row insertions or deletions. This makes it a popular choice for Excel users seeking greater flexibility and precision in their data retrieval tasks.

Syntax and Arguments

The INDEX function returns the value of a cell in a specific row and column within a given array:

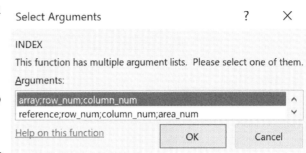

=INDEX(array, row_num, [col_num])

- **array**: The range of cells you want to search.
- **row_num**: The row number in the array from which to retrieve the value.
- **col_num**: Optional. The column number in the array from which to retrieve the value.

The MATCH function searches for a specific value in a range and returns its relative position:

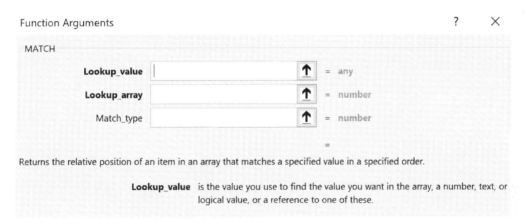

=MATCH(lookup_value, lookup_array, [match_type])

- **lookup_value**: The value you want to find.
- **lookup_array**: The range of cells containing the value you want to find.
- **match_type**: Optional. The type of match to find (exact match, less than, or greater than).

When used together, MATCH finds the position of the lookup_value, and INDEX returns the value at that position:

=INDEX(array, MATCH(lookup_value, lookup_array, [match_type]))

Example in Context – For instance, if you have a table of employee IDs in column A and their salaries in column B, you can find the salary of an employee with a specific ID as follows:

=INDEX(B2:B10, MATCH("EMP123", A2:A10, 0))

This formula first uses MATCH to find the row number where "EMP123" appears in the range A2:A10. Then, INDEX uses that row number to retrieve the corresponding salary from the range B2:B10.

Practical Applications

The INDEX/MATCH combination is incredibly versatile:

- *Multi-Column Searches*: Unlike VLOOKUP, which can only search to the right, INDEX/MATCH can look in any direction.

- *Dynamic Ranges*: If your data range changes frequently, INDEX/MATCH is less likely to break than VLOOKUP or HLOOKUP.

You can also use INDEX/MATCH with other functions like SUM, AVERAGE, or even within array formulas for more complex data manipulation tasks.

Understanding Pivot Tables: Creation and customization

Pivot Tables are a powerful tool in Excel for analyzing data. They help you explore large datasets and discover trends. You could be a sales manager looking to dissect quarterly revenue, an inventory analyst tracking stock levels, or a researcher sifting through survey data, Pivot Tables provide a solid framework for data manipulation and analysis.

Creating a Pivot Table

Step 1: Preparing Your Data

Before you even think about creating a Pivot Table, you need to ensure your data is clean and well-organized. Excel prefers data in a tabular format, where each column represents a different variable, and each row represents an individual record. Once your data is in good shape, select the range of cells you wish to analyze.

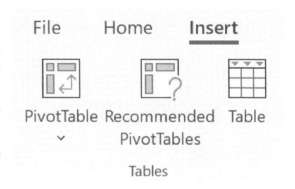

Step 2: Initiating the Pivot Table

To create a Pivot Table, go to the 'Insert' tab on the Excel ribbon and click the 'PivotTable' button. A dialog box will pop up, prompting you to confirm your data range and specify where you'd like the Pivot Table to be placed—either in a new worksheet or an existing one.

Step 3: Building Your Pivot Table

After clicking 'OK' in the dialog box, Excel will generate a blank Pivot Table and display the 'PivotTable Fields' panel on the right side of the screen. This panel is where the magic happens. You'll see a list of all the columns from your selected data range, and you can drag these into four different areas:

- Rows: Fields placed here will appear as row labels in the Pivot Table.

- Columns: Fields here will show up as column headers.

- Values: This area is where your data gets summarized. You can choose to sum, average, count, or perform other calculations on these fields.

- Filters: Fields placed here allow you to filter the entire Pivot Table based on the selected criteria.

Sample sales data

Date	Color	Region	Units	Sales
3-Jan-16	Brown	West	1	$11,00
13-Jan-16	Yellow	South	8	$96,00
21-Jan-16	Green	West	2	$26,00
30-Jan-16	Yellow	North	7	$84,00
7-Feb-16	Green	North	8	$104,00
13-Feb-16	Brown	South	2	$22,00
21-Feb-16	Yellow	East	5	$60,00
1-Mar-16	Green	West	2	$26,00
13-Mar-16	Yellow	East	8	$96,00
23-Mar-16	Yellow	North	7	$84,00
28-Mar-16	Green	West	2	$26,00

Row Labels	Sum of Units	Sum of Sales
Brown	43	473
gen	1	11
feb	2	22
apr	14	154
mag	5	55
giu	3	33
lug	8	88
set	10	110
Green	43	559
Yellow	84	1008
Grand Total	**170**	**2040**

Customizing Your Pivot Table

Once you've built the basic structure of your Pivot Table, you can start customizing it to better suit your needs.

Sorting and Filtering

Sorting and filtering are fundamental operations you can perform on a Pivot Table, much like you would on a standard Excel table. To sort data, right-click on a cell within the column you wish to sort and choose 'Sort A to Z' or 'Sort Z to A'.

For filtering, the process is equally simple. Each column header in the Pivot Table has a drop-down arrow that lets you filter out specific values or a range of values. When you're dealing with large datasets and need to focus on particular subsets of data, this feature is there for you.

Calculated Fields

One of the standout features of Pivot Tables is the ability to add calculated fields. These are custom fields that you can create to perform calculations based on the existing columns in your Pivot Table. For instance, if you have columns for 'Revenue' and 'Expenses', you could create a calculated field for 'Profit' by subtracting Expenses from Revenue. To add a calculated field, go to the 'PivotTable Analyze' tab and select 'Fields, Items, & Sets', then choose 'Calculated Field'. A dialog box will appear where you can name your new field and enter the formula for the calculation.

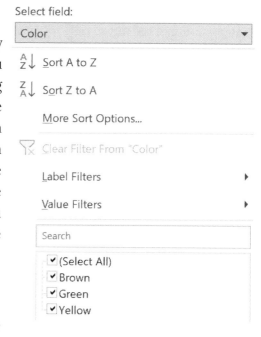

Grouping Data

Grouping is another powerful feature that allows you to segment data in meaningful ways. For example, if you have a date field, you can group data by month, quarter, or year to get a more aggregated view of your data. To group data, right-click on a cell within the column you wish to group and select 'Group'. A dialog box will appear, offering various grouping options based on the data type.

Formatting

Pivot Tables also support conditional formatting, which can be a valuable tool for highlighting specific data points or trends. To apply conditional formatting, select the cells you wish to format, go to the 'Home' tab, and choose 'Conditional Formatting'. From here, you can select from a variety of options, including color scales, data bars, and icon sets, to make your data stand out.

Practical Applications

Sales Reports - Pivot Tables are excellent for summarizing sales data. You can easily create a report that breaks down sales by region, product category, or individual salesperson. This enables managers to quickly identify high-performing products or regions and make data-driven decisions.

Inventory Management - In the context of inventory management, Pivot Tables can offer a granular view of stock levels across multiple locations. You can set up a Pivot Table to show current stock, incoming shipments, and sales rates, allowing you to forecast future stock requirements accurately.

Survey Analysis - For those dealing with survey data, Pivot Tables can aggregate responses to identify trends or patterns. Are you looking at customer satisfaction levels or employee engagement? A well-structured Pivot Table can yield swift comprehension of extensive survey data.

For those who want to go beyond the basics, Excel offers several advanced customization options, including the ability to create Pivot Charts, slicers for easier data filtering, and even integrating Pivot Tables with Power Query for more complex data manipulation tasks.

Advanced Conditional Formatting Techniques

While basic conditional formatting can highlight cells based on simple conditions like "greater than" or "less than," advanced techniques enable you to take your data visualization to the next level.

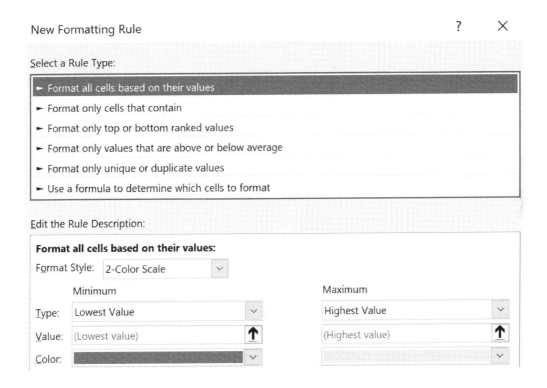

Formula-Based Conditional Formatting

One of the most potent advanced techniques is formula-based conditional formatting, which allows you to apply formatting based on a custom formula. For example, you could highlight cells in a column where the value is above the average of all the values in that column.

To apply formula-based conditional formatting:

1. Select the range of cells you want to format.

2. Go to the 'Home' tab and click on 'Conditional Formatting'.

3. Choose 'New Rule' and then select 'Use a formula to determine which cells to format'.

4. Enter your formula and define the formatting options.

Conditional Formatting with Multiple Conditions

You can also apply multiple conditions to a single cell or range of cells. For instance, you might want to highlight sales figures that are both above average and have increased from the previous month.

To do this:

1. Apply the first condition using the standard conditional formatting options.

2. Go back to 'Conditional Formatting' and choose 'Manage Rules'.

3. Click on 'New Rule' to add another condition.

4. Make sure both rules are checked in the 'Manage Rules' dialog box.

Data Bars

Data bars fill the background of a cell with a color, the length of which represents the cell's value. Using them, you can quickly identify higher or lower values in a range of data. For example, in a column of monthly sales figures, longer bars would instantly indicate months with higher sales.

To apply data bars:

1. Select the range of cells you want to format.

2. Go to the 'Home' tab and click on 'Conditional Formatting'.

3. Choose 'Data Bars' and select a color scheme.

Color Scales

Color scales apply a two- or three-color gradient to a range of cells based on their values. This can be useful for spotting trends or anomalies in a dataset. For instance, you could use a red-to-green color scale to indicate low-to-high performance metrics.

To apply color scales:

1. Select the range of cells you want to format.

2. Go to the 'Home' tab and click on 'Conditional Formatting'.

3. Choose 'Color Scales' and select a gradient.

Icon Sets

Icon sets offer a way to add a layer of visual interpretation to your data. For example, you could use arrows to indicate an increase, stability, or decrease in monthly sales figures.

To apply icon sets:

1. Select the range of cells you want to format.

2. Go to the 'Home' tab and click on 'Conditional Formatting'.

3. Choose 'Icon Sets' and select the set that best suits your data.

Blending Techniques

The true power of advanced conditional formatting lies in the ability to blend different techniques. For instance, you could use a formula to set a condition, such as highlighting cells where sales have increased by more than 10%. Then, you could add an icon set to those highlighted cells to indicate the degree of increase.

To blend techniques:

1. Apply the first technique, such as a formula-based rule.

2. Without deselecting the range, go back to 'Conditional Formatting' and choose another technique, like 'Icon Sets'.

3. In the 'Manage Rules' dialog, ensure both rules are active and set the order of precedence if necessary.

Array Formulas and Functions

Unlike standard formulas, which process individual values, array formulas can process entire ranges of data at once. This makes them incredibly efficient for complex calculations that involve matching, summing, or averaging multiple sets of numbers.

The utility of array formulas lies in their ability to simplify workflows. Instead of writing several different formulas to achieve a particular result, you can often accomplish the same task with a single array formula. This not only makes your Excel sheets easier to manage but also reduces the likelihood of errors that can occur when dealing with multiple formulas.

Basic Array Functions

SUMPRODUCT

The SUMPRODUCT function is one of the most commonly used array functions in Excel. It takes multiple arrays of numbers and multiplies corresponding elements in the given arrays, and then sums up those products.

Syntax: **=SUMPRODUCT(array1, [array2], [array3], ...)**

Example: Suppose you have two arrays, one representing the quantity of items sold (A1:A3 = [2, 3, 4]) and the other representing the price of those items (B1:B3 = [10, 20, 30]). To calculate the total revenue, you could use SUMPRODUCT like this: **=SUMPRODUCT(A1:A3, B1:B3)** This would result in (2*10) + (3*20) + (4*30) = 20 + 60 + 120 = 200.

=SUMPRODUCT(D3:D8;E3:E8)		
D	E	F
1	2	100
3	4	
5	6	
7	8	

TRANSPOSE

=TRANSPOSE(D3:D6)			
D	E	F	G
52	228	199	783
52			
228			
199			
783			

The TRANSPOSE function allows you to switch the rows and columns with each other, effectively rotating your array data.

Syntax: **=TRANSPOSE(array)**

Example: If you have an array in A1:C2 where the first row is [1, 2, 3] and the second row is [4, 5, 6], using TRANSPOSE would change its orientation. The new array would have its first column as [1, 4] and its second column as [2, 5], and so on.

FREQUENCY

The FREQUENCY function is used to count how often values occur within a range of values. This is particularly useful for statistical analysis and data distribution studies.

Syntax: **=FREQUENCY(data_array, bins_array)**

Example: Suppose you have a dataset of exam scores in A1:A10, and you want to know how many scores fall into certain grade bins (e.g., 60-69, 70-79, 80-89, 90-100). You could set up your bins in B1:B4 ([69, 79, 89, 100]) and then use **FREQUENCY(A1:A10, B1:B4)** to get the count of scores in each bin.

Creating Array Formulas

Array formulas in Excel offer capabilities that go far beyond regular formulas. While standard formulas in Excel operate on one cell at a time, array formulas allow you to perform calculations across entire ranges all at once. This enables you to carry out complex data analysis and manipulation using a single array formula rather than many individual formulas.

One major benefit of array formulas is their ability to simultaneously execute functions like sums, averages, and counts across cell ranges. For example, you could calculate the total or average of sales data for an entire year in one step. With regular Excel formulas, you would need to create individual formulas for each month or day. The array formula condenses this workflow tremendously.

In addition to statistical operations, array formulas open up other options like transposing or transforming your data sets. Manipulations that would require copying and pasting ranges or introducing helper columns can be achieved within the array formula itself. This removes the need for all the incremental regular formulas.

Entering an array formula is slightly different from entering a regular formula. Here's how to do it:

	A	B	C	D	E
1	1	2		44	
2	3	4			
3	5	6			

D1: `{=SUM(A1:A3 * B1:B3)}`

1. **Select the Cell Range**: First, select the range of cells where you want the array formula to apply. This is especially important for functions that will return multiple values.

2. **Type the Formula**: Next, type your array formula into the formula bar just as you would with a regular formula. Do not press Enter yet.

3. **Use Ctrl+Shift+Enter**: Instead of pressing Enter, you must press Ctrl+Shift+Enter simultaneously. This tells Excel that you're entering an array formula. You'll know it's been entered correctly when you see curly braces {} appear around your formula in the formula bar.

For instance, if you're entering a simple array formula like **=SUM(A1:A3 * B1:B3)**, you would type it into the formula bar and then press Ctrl+Shift+Enter. The formula bar will display it as **{=SUM(A1:A3 * B1:B3)}**.

Let's look at some basic examples to understand how array formulas work:

- *Sum of Squares of a Range*: Suppose you have a range of numbers in A1:A5, and you want to find the sum of their squares. You could use the array formula **=SUM(A1:A5^2)**. After typing this formula, press Ctrl+Shift+Enter.

- *Average of Product of Two Ranges*: If you have two ranges, A1:A3 and B1:B3, and you want to find the average of their product, you could use the formula **=AVERAGE(A1:A3 * B1:B3)**. Again, remember to press Ctrl+Shift+Enter.

- *Count of Values Greater Than Average*: Let's say you have a range of numbers in A1:A10, and you want to count how many values are greater than the average of this range. You could use the formula **=SUM(IF(A1:A10>AVERAGE(A1:A10), 1, 0))**. Press Ctrl+Shift+Enter after typing the formula.

- *The sum of the Smallest Three Numbers*: If you have a range A1:A10 and you want to sum the smallest three numbers, you could use the formula **=SUM(SMALL(A1:A10, {1,2,3}))**. Press Ctrl+Shift+Enter to finalize the formula.

Dynamic Arrays and Spill Range

Dynamic arrays and the spill range concept are game-changing features in Excel that bring a new level of power and flexibility to spreadsheet calculations. Those who regularly work with large datasets and complex formulas will appreciate these features. Let's find out what these terms mean and how they can be utilized effectively.

In traditional Excel formulas, the output is usually a single value that populates a single cell. However, dynamic arrays allow a formula to return multiple values that "spill" over into a range of cells. This is incredibly useful for functions that naturally produce multiple results. For example, if you're using a function to find all instances of a particular value in a range, a dynamic array can return all of them at once, filling multiple cells.

Dynamic arrays are automatically resizable, meaning they adjust the output range based on the number of values returned. This makes your spreadsheets more efficient and reduces the need for manual adjustments.

The Spill Range Concept

The term "spill range" refers to the range of cells that a dynamic array formula fills with its multiple outputs. When you enter a dynamic array formula, Excel identifies the necessary spill range and populates it with the formula's output values. If something is blocking the spill range (e.g., existing data or formulas in the cells where the output would spill), Excel will return a **#SPILL!** Error.

The spill range is dynamic, meaning it will automatically adjust if the number of output values changes. For example, if your dynamic array formula is set to list all the employees in a department and a new employee is added, the spill range will automatically expand to include this new data.

Practical Applications

1. *Filtering Data:* You have a list of sales transactions, and you want to filter out only those that are above a certain value. You could use the **FILTER** function, which is designed to work with dynamic arrays, to do this. The formula =**FILTER(A2:B10, B2:B10>1000)** would return all transactions over $1000 and spill the results into a dynamic range.

2. *Sorting Data:* The **SORT** function can be used to sort a range of data in ascending or descending order. For example, =**SORT(A1:A10)** would sort the range A1:A10 in ascending order and spill the sorted list into a new range.

=SORT(C2:C10)

C	D
Transactions	
$350,00	$147,00
$1.200,00	$256,00
$498,00	$350,00
$2.070,00	$498,00
$1.350,00	$620,00
$620,00	$1.090,00
$147,00	$1.200,00
$256,00	$1.350,00
$1.090,00	$2.070,00

3. *Unique Values:* If you have a list with duplicate values and you want a list of unique values, you can use the **UNIQUE** function. The formula =**UNIQUE(A1:A10)** will spill a list of unique values into a dynamic range.

4. *Multiple Criteria Lookups:* Dynamic arrays make it easier to perform lookups based on various criteria. For example, you could use the **XLOOKUP** function in combination with dynamic arrays to find data that meets several conditions.

Array Formulas with Conditional Logic

Array formulas paired with conditional logic can bring a new level of sophistication to your Excel spreadsheets. They allow you to perform complex calculations based on certain conditions, making your data analysis more nuanced and targeted. One of the most common functions used in this context is the **IF** function.

Using IF with Array Formulas

The **IF** function is often used to test a condition and return one value if the condition is true and another value if it's false. When used in an array formula, the **IF** function can evaluate multiple conditions at once, returning an array of results rather than a single value.

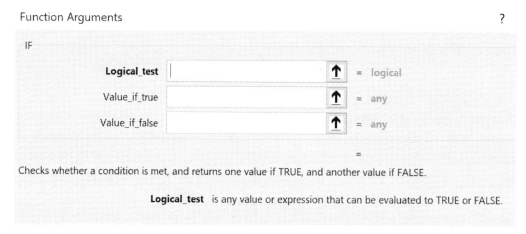

Syntax for IF in array formulas: =**IF(array_condition, array_if_true, array_if_false)**

Here, **array_condition** is an array of logical conditions, **array_if_true** is the array of values to return if the condition is true, and **array_if_false** is the array of values to return if the condition is false.

Example: Summing Only the Values That Meet a Certain Condition

You have a list of sales figures in column A (from A1 to A10), and you want to sum only those greater than $1,000. You could use an array formula with **IF** and **SUM** like this:

=SUM(IF(A1:A10 > 1000, A1:A10, 0))

Here's what happens:

1. **IF(A1:A10 > 1000, A1:A10, 0)** checks each cell in the range A1:A10 to see if it's greater than $1,000.

2. If a cell's value is greater than $1,000, that value is included in an array.

3. If a cell's value is not greater than $1,000, a zero is included in the array.

4. Finally, **SUM** adds up the values in the array.

Note: To enter this as an array formula, you would press Ctrl+Shift+Enter (not just Enter).

Best Practices and Practical Applications

Array formulas, especially those with conditional logic, can be computationally intensive. This is particularly true for large datasets. Each condition in an array formula is evaluated for every cell in the specified range, which can slow down Excel's performance. Therefore, it's crucial to be mindful of the computational load when using complex array formulas.

When to Use and When Not to Use Array Formulas

Array formulas are powerful but are not always the best tool for every job. Here are some guidelines:

- Use When: You need to perform complex calculations that involve multiple conditions or multiple ranges.

- Avoid When: Your dataset is extremely large, or you're performing a simple calculation that can be done with a standard formula.

Practical Applications

Here are some real-world situations where array formulas with conditional logic can be beneficial:

- *Financial Analysis*: For example, you could use an array formula to calculate the average return of stocks with a certain risk level.

- *Inventory Management*: Array formulas can help you calculate the total value of items below a certain stock level, allowing for targeted restocking.

- *Data Cleaning*: When dealing with messy data, array formulas can help you filter out or correct anomalies based on specific conditions.

- *Human Resources*: You could use array formulas to automatically calculate bonuses for employees who meet or exceed certain performance metrics.

Linking, Embedding, and Importing Data

In the modern business environment, data rarely resides in a single location. You often need to pull in data from various sources, be it another Excel workbook, a database, or even a website. Excel provides robust features for linking, embedding, and importing data, each with its strengths and use cases. Let's explore each one in detail.

Linking Data

Linking allows you to connect to data in another workbook. Any changes made to the source data are automatically reflected in the workbook where the data is linked.

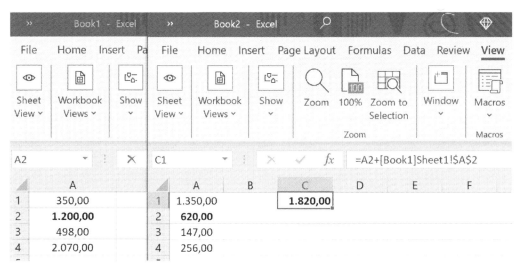

How to Do It:

    1. Open both the source and destination workbooks.

    2. In the destination workbook, select the cell where you want the linked data to appear.

    3. Type = and then navigate to the source workbook and select the cell you want to link.

    4. Press Enter.

Use Cases:

- Financial reports that pull data from various departmental spreadsheets.
- Dashboards that aggregate data from multiple sources.

Embedding Data

Embedding involves inserting data from another file into your workbook. Unlike linking, the data is not updated if the source file changes.

How to Do It:

    1. Go to the 'Insert' tab.

    2. Choose 'Object' and then browse to the file you wish to embed.

    3. Click 'OK'.

Use-Cases:

- Inserting a static chart or table that doesn't require updates.
- Including supplementary information like PDFs.

Importing Data

Importing data means bringing in data from external sources like databases, text files, or websites.

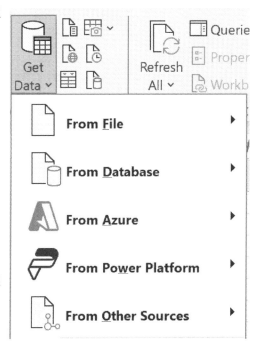

How to Do It:

1. Go to the 'Data' tab.

2. Choose 'Get Data' and select your data source.

3. Follow the prompts to import the data.

Use-Cases:

- Importing sales data from a CRM system.

- Loading data from a CSV file for data cleaning and analysis.

Best Practices

Data integrity refers to the accuracy and consistency of data. When you're linking or importing data from external sources, the data must be correct and reliable.

Incorrect data can lead to flawed analyses and misguided business decisions. For example, if you're linking to a sales database, inaccuracies in the sales figures could result in incorrect revenue forecasts.

How to Ensure It:

- Double-check the source data before linking or importing.

- If possible, set up automated data validation checks.

- Regularly update linked or imported data to ensure it reflects the most current information.

Performance in this context refers to how quickly and smoothly your Excel workbook operates.

Embedding large files or linking to complex data sources can slow down your workbook, making it cumbersome to use. This can be especially problematic for files that multiple team members need to access simultaneously.

How to Manage It:

- Be selective about what you embed; try to keep file sizes as small as possible.

- For linked data, consider using Excel's 'Data Model' feature to improve performance.

- Use Excel's 'Query' options to pull in only the necessary data when linking or importing.

Updates - This refers to keeping your linked data up-to-date and ensuring that the source files are accessible. Outdated or inaccessible data can lead to incorrect analyses and may also result in 'broken' links within your workbook.

How to Maintain It:

- Regularly check that the source files for linked data are accessible and up-to-date.

- Use Excel's 'Refresh' feature to update linked or imported data.

- Set reminders to review and update embedded objects that may have newer versions.

Chapter Six

DAY 6: ADVANCED EXCEL FEATURES

Today, we'll explore advanced Excel features that can significantly enhance your data analysis and reporting skills. While earlier chapters covered Excel's core features, this chapter goes further by introducing tools and techniques for automating tasks, managing complex data, and creating dynamic visualizations.

We'll begin with collaborative editing, a feature that allows multiple users to work on the same Excel file simultaneously, boosting teamwork and productivity. Then, we'll delve into Macros and VBA (Visual Basic for Applications) for automating actions, saving time, and reducing errors.

Next, I'll guide you through recording and editing macros, providing the basics of automation. We'll also look into Power Query and Power Pivot, powerful tools for data manipulation and analysis, offering ease in handling large datasets and complex calculations.

You'll learn how to manage multidimensional data with 3D references and tables, enabling comprehensive analyses across multiple worksheets. Finally, we'll explore advanced charting techniques to create more insightful and engaging data visualizations.

Collaborative Editing and Co-Authoring

Collaborative editing is a feature that enables multiple users to work on the same Excel file simultaneously. In a team setting, this is essential for several reasons. It allows for real-time updates, meaning that changes made by one team member are instantly visible to others. This immediate sharing of information enhances productivity, streamlines workflows, and minimizes the risk of errors or duplications that can occur when multiple versions of the same file are circulated.

Excel offers co-authoring capabilities that take collaborative editing a step further by making real-time collaboration possible. With co-authoring, team members can work together seamlessly, whether they are in the same office or spread across different locations. Teams that require quick decision-making based on data can definitely appreciate this feature as it ensures that everyone is always on the same page.

Setting Up for Collaboration

To take advantage of Excel's co-authoring capabilities, the first step is to save your Excel file in a location that can be accessed by all team members. This could be a cloud storage service like OneDrive or SharePoint, or a collaboration platform like Microsoft Teams.

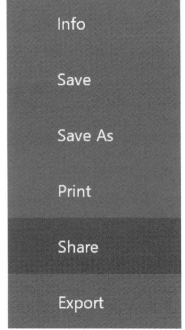

- OneDrive: Simply upload your Excel file to a OneDrive folder and then share the folder or file link with your team.

- SharePoint: If your organization uses SharePoint, save the file in a SharePoint library. This will also allow you to use additional features like version history and advanced permissions settings.

- Microsoft Teams: If you're using Teams, you can upload the Excel file directly into a channel. Team members in that channel will automatically have access to the file.

Once the file is in a shared location, the next step is to set up permissions. Permissions control who can view or edit the file. Here's how to manage them:

- OneDrive and SharePoint: After uploading the file, click on the 'Share' button. You can then enter the email addresses of the team members you want to collaborate with. You'll also have the option to allow them to edit or only view the file.

- Microsoft Teams: Permissions are generally managed at the channel level. If a team member has access to the channel where the file is uploaded, they'll have access to the file as well. However, you can also set specific permissions by clicking on the file within Teams and then selecting 'Manage Access.'

Real-Time Co-Authoring

Co-authoring allows multiple users to work on the same Excel sheet simultaneously without locking out any part of the sheet. Each user can edit cells, input data, and even run calculations in real-time, and the changes are instantly visible to all other collaborators.

When you're co-authoring an Excel document, the user interface provides several visual cues to indicate who else is working on the document with you:

- *Colored Cursors*: Each collaborator is assigned a unique color. When they are working on the sheet, you will see a colored cell border or cursor moving in real-time, representing their actions.

- *Name Tags*: Hovering over the colored cursor will display a name tag, showing you exactly who is making changes. This is especially useful in documents with multiple collaborators.

- *Presence Indicators*: In the upper-right corner of the Excel window, you'll often see icons or profile pictures representing each person who has the document open. Clicking on these icons will give you more details, such as their contact information or even a chat option to communicate without leaving Excel.

- *Real-Time Updates*: As collaborators make changes, you'll witness those modifications happening in real time. This encompasses not only data entry but also formula calculations, formatting adjustments, and even comments or notes added to cells.

Conflict Resolution

When multiple authors are working on the same Excel sheet, there's a possibility of conflicting changes. For example, two users might try to edit the same cell simultaneously. Excel has built-in mechanisms to handle such conflicts to ensure data integrity.

In case of a conflict, Excel will display a "Merge Changes" dialog box. This dialog box will list all the conflicting changes and present options for resolving them. You can choose to keep your changes, accept someone else's changes, or even merge the changes manually. Once you've made your selections, clicking "OK" will apply the resolution and update the sheet for all collaborators.

Commenting and Communication

Excel's comment feature allows for contextual discussions right within the sheet. You can add comments to specific cells, making it easier to discuss data points, formulas, or any other aspect of the sheet. To add a comment, simply right-click on a cell and choose "New Comment," or use the "Review" tab in the Ribbon and select "New Comment."

For more targeted communication, Excel supports @mentions within comments. By typing "@" followed by a team member's name, you can directly notify them about the comment. They will receive a notification and can quickly navigate to the relevant cell to view the comment and respond.

Version History

Excel's version history feature is a lifesaver when you need to revert to a previous version of the document or review changes made over time. To access version history, go to the "File" tab and select "Info." From there, you'll see an option for "Version History," which will display a sidebar showing different saved versions of the document. If you're using OneDrive or SharePoint, you can also find the "Version History" option by right-clicking on the file.

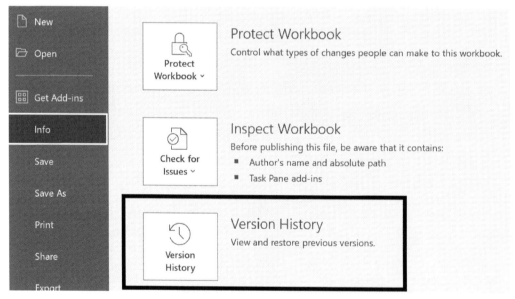

Once you've accessed the version history, you can click on any of the listed versions to open it in a new window. This lets you review changes, see who made them, and what was modified. If you find that you need to revert to a previous version, there's usually an option to "Restore" that version, which will replace the current file with the selected older version.

Version history is crucial for maintaining the integrity of collaborative documents. It provides a safety net, allowing you to undo changes that may have been made accidentally or without full team consensus. It also adds a layer of accountability, as you can see who made what changes and when. This is particularly useful in team settings where multiple people are editing the document, and decisions may need to be traced back for clarification or auditing purposes.

Introduction to Macros and VBA

Macros in Excel are more than just a set of automated steps; they are a powerful tool that can transform your workflow. At their core, macros are sequences of commands or actions that are either recorded or manually programmed to execute specific tasks automatically. They function like a script for Excel, enabling you to automate a wide range of activities, from simple tasks like data entry to more complex operations like data analysis. The language behind these macros is called Visual Basic for Applications (VBA), a programming language developed by Microsoft for automation in their Office suite of products.

The Benefits of Using Macros

Time-Saving - One of the most convincing reasons to use macros is their time-saving aspect. Automation through macros can drastically reduce the time spent on repetitive tasks. Let's say you have to generate weekly reports that involve multiple steps like sorting, filtering, and calculations; a macro can do all these steps for you, saving a significant amount of time compared to manual execution.

Accuracy - Human error is a constant risk in any task that involves repetition. By automating these tasks, macros eliminate the possibility of mistakes that can occur from manual input. This ensures that the task is performed consistently and accurately each time, which is especially crucial in tasks that involve financial calculations or data analysis.

Ease of Use - Macros are not just for Excel experts. Once a macro is created, it can be run by anyone with basic Excel skills. This democratizes the ability to perform complex tasks, making it easier to distribute work within a team without requiring everyone to have the same level of expertise.

Diving Deeper into VBA

Visual Basic for Applications (VBA) is the backbone of Excel macros. While the macro recorder in Excel captures your actions in VBA code, understanding VBA itself allows you to go beyond the limitations of the macro recorder. With VBA, you can create more complex and customized functions, automate decision-making processes, interact with other applications, and even create your own Excel functions.

VBA is an event-driven programming language, meaning it executes code in response to specific events like a button click or a cell change. This allows for dynamic and interactive functionalities that can adapt to user actions or data changes.

Basic Automation

The Basics of Recording a Macro

Recording a macro is your gateway to automating repetitive tasks in Excel. It's an excellent first step for those unfamiliar with automation or VBA (Visual Basic for Applications). The process is straightforward, but each step has its nuances that are worth understanding. Here's a detailed guide on how to record a basic macro in Excel:

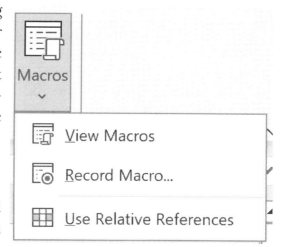

Step 1: Open the Macro Dialog

- How: Navigate to the 'View' tab in the Excel ribbon. Locate the 'Macros' group and click on the 'Record Macro' option from the dropdown menu.

- Why: This is where Excel allows you to initiate the macro recording process. The 'View' tab is your hub for macro-related activities.

Step 2: Name Your Macro

- How: A dialog box will appear, prompting you to name your macro.

- Why: Naming your macro is crucial for identification, especially when you have multiple macros. Choose a name that is descriptive of the task the macro will perform. Avoid using spaces or special characters, as they can cause errors in VBA.

Step 3: Assign a Shortcut Key (Optional)

- How: In the same dialog box, you'll see an option to assign a shortcut key.

- Why: A shortcut key allows you to run the macro without navigating through menus. However, be cautious not to overwrite existing Excel shortcuts, as this can disrupt your workflow.

Step 4: Decide Where to Save the Macro

- How: You'll be asked where you want to store the macro. The options are the current workbook, a new workbook, or a personal macro workbook.

- Why: The location where you save the macro affects its accessibility. Saving it in the current workbook means it will only be available in that specific file. A personal macro workbook makes the macro available every time you open Excel.

Step 5: Start Recording

- How: After filling out the dialog box, click 'OK' to commence the recording.

- Why: This action signals Excel to start capturing all your subsequent steps, translating them into VBA code in the background.

Step 6: Perform the Actions

- How: Execute the steps you want to automate in your Excel worksheet.

- Why: Excel is now in recording mode, capturing each action you perform. These actions will be translated into VBA code, which will be the backbone of your macro.

Step 7: Stop Recording

- How: Once you've completed the steps, navigate back to the 'Macros' group under the 'View' tab and click 'Stop Recording.'

- Why: This action halts the recording process, and your macro is now ready for use. Excel will have converted your actions into a VBA script that can be run to automate the task you just performed.

Editing a Recorded Macro

Recording a macro is just the beginning; you may find that you need to tweak or modify it later. This is where having a fundamental grasp of VBA (Visual Basic for Applications) becomes essential.

Here's a step-by-step guide on how to edit a recorded macro in Excel:

Step 1: Open the VBA Editor

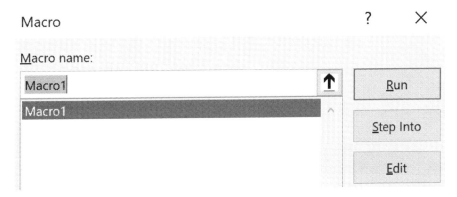

Go to the 'View' tab in the Excel ribbon, click on 'Macros,' and then select 'View Macros.' A dialog box will appear listing all available macros. Choose the macro you wish to edit and click the 'Edit' button.

The VBA Editor is the environment where you can view and modify the VBA code that makes up your macro. Accessing it is the first step in the editing process.

Step 2: Understand the Code

Once the VBA Editor opens, you'll see the VBA code that was generated when you recorded the macro. Take a moment to review it.

Understanding the structure of the VBA code will help you identify which parts need editing. Each line or block of code corresponds to an action you performed during the recording. Familiarizing yourself with the code makes the editing process smoother.

```
Book1 - Module1 (Code)
(General)                                               Macro1

Sub Macro1()
'
' Macro1 Macro
'

    Range("G5").Select
    ActiveCell.FormulaR1C1 = "123"
    Range("G6").Select
    ActiveCell.FormulaR1C1 = "=R[-1]C*5"
    Range("G7").Select
End Sub
```

Step 3: Make Edits

Locate the section of the code you want to modify. Make your changes, paying close attention to the syntax and structure of the code.

VBA is sensitive to syntax errors, and even a small mistake can cause the macro to malfunction. Therefore, it's crucial to make edits carefully. If you're unsure about a change, it's wise to copy the original code to a separate location as a backup.

Step 4: Test the Macro

After making your edits, close the VBA Editor and return to Excel. Run the macro to see if it performs as expected.

Testing is a critical step in the editing process. It ensures that your changes have the desired effect and that you haven't introduced any errors into the code. Always test on sample data to mitigate the risk of unintended consequences.

Step 5: Save Changes

If the macro performs as expected after testing, go ahead and save your changes. If you've stored the macro in your personal macro workbook, it will be available whenever you open Excel.

Saving the macro finalizes your edits, making them a permanent part of the macro's functionality. Make sure you're happy with the macro's performance before saving.

Practical Tips

Editing macros is not just about changing the VBA code; it's also about making that code strong, understandable, and efficient. Here are some practical tips to consider when you're editing macros in Excel:

Use Comments for Clarity - In VBA, you can add comments by typing an apostrophe (') followed by the comment text. The VBA engine ignores these comments when running the code.

Comments are very important for understanding the purpose and functionality of different sections of your code. They serve as in-line documentation that can help both you and others who might work on this macro in the future. For example, you could write a comment like *'This line sorts the data'* before a sorting command.

Implement Error Handling - VBA allows for error-handling routines using commands like **On Error Resume Next** or **On Error GoTo Label**. Insert these commands at the beginning of your macro or before a section where an error might occur.

Error handling can make your macro more robust and user-friendly. Without it, any error would cause the macro to stop abruptly, which could be confusing for the user. With error handling, you can control what happens when an error occurs—whether that's skipping the problematic step, displaying a custom error message, or even rolling back changes.

Be Cautious with Loops - When using loops like **For**, **While**, or **Do Until**, always make sure to include an exit condition. This could be a maximum number of iterations or a specific condition that, when met, will break the loop.

Loops are powerful but can be dangerous if not controlled. An infinite loop (one that never meets its exit condition) can cause Excel to freeze or crash. Therefore, including a reliable exit condition in your loops is crucial. For instance, if you're looping through rows in a dataset, you might include a condition to exit the loop when an empty row is encountered.

Introduction to Excel Power Query and Power Pivot

Power Query and Power Pivot are two of Excel's most potent tools for data analysis and business intelligence. While they serve different purposes, they are often used in conjunction to transform raw data into meaningful insights. Here, I would like to provide a comprehensive introduction to these advanced Excel features, explaining what they are, why you should use them, and how they can revolutionize your data analysis workflow.

What is Power Query?

Power Query is a data connection technology that enables you to connect, transform, and combine data from various sources. It's essentially a data preparation engine that allows you to clean, reshape, and aggregate data before bringing it into Excel or Power Pivot.

Key Features of Power Query

- Data Import: Import data from multiple sources, including databases, Excel files, web services, etc.

- Data Transformation: Clean and transform your data by removing duplicates, replacing values, splitting columns, and so on.

- Query Editor: A user-friendly interface that lets you perform complex data manipulations without needing to know SQL or other query languages.

What is Power Pivot?

Power Pivot is an in-memory data modeling component that lets you create data models, establish relationships, and build calculations. It's useful for managing large datasets that would be cumbersome in traditional Excel sheets.

Key Features of Power Pivot:

- Data Modeling: Create relationships between tables, define hierarchies, and build calculated columns and measures.

- DAX (Data Analysis Expressions): A formula language that allows you to create complex calculations and aggregations.

- PivotTables on Steroids: Power Pivot enables you to create more advanced and dynamic PivotTables, leveraging the data model you've built.

Why Use Power Query and Power Pivot?

Efficiency - One of the most compelling reasons to use Power Query and Power Pivot is the efficiency they bring to your data analysis workflow. Power Query allows you to automate the data preparation process, eliminating the need for manual data cleaning. This is particularly beneficial for large datasets or repetitive tasks you perform regularly. On the other hand, Power Pivot is optimized for performance, enabling you to work with millions of rows of data without slowing down your computer.

Data Integrity - Maintaining the accuracy and consistency of your data is crucial for reliable analysis. Power Query and Power Pivot help you achieve this by centralizing your data transformations and calculations. In Power Query, once you define a set of transformations, they are applied consistently every time you refresh your data. Similarly, in Power Pivot, calculations and relationships are defined at the data model level, ensuring uniformity across all your analyses.

Advanced Analysis - Excel is a powerful tool, but it has its limitations, especially when it comes to complex data manipulations and calculations. This is where Power Query and Power Pivot come in. They extend Excel's capabilities, allowing you to perform advanced analytics that would be either cumbersome or impossible using Excel alone. With features like DAX formulas in Power Pivot and advanced query functions in Power Query, you can dig deeper into your data and extract more meaningful insights.

How to Use Power Query and Power Pivot Together

Data Import - The first step in using Power Query and Power Pivot together is importing your data. Power Query offers a wide range of connectors for different data sources, including SQL databases, Excel files, and even web services. Once you've connected to your data source, Power Query will display a preview, allowing you to select the specific tables or fields you want to import.

Data Cleaning - After importing your data, you'll likely need to clean and transform it to suit your analysis needs. Power Query offers a user-friendly interface for this, complete with different transformation options. It enables you to eliminate duplicates, filter rows, split or merge columns, and perform many other actions through simple point-and-click operations.

Load to Data Model - Once your data is clean and well-structured, you can load it into Power Pivot's data model. This is as simple as clicking the 'Close & Load' button in Power Query and choosing to load the data to the Power Pivot model. This action will make the data available for more advanced manipulations and calculations in Power Pivot.

Modeling and Calculations - With your data loaded into Power Pivot, you can now start building your data model. This involves creating relationships between tables, defining hierarchies, and adding calculated columns and measures. Power Pivot uses a formula language called DAX (Data Analysis Expressions) for these calculations, allowing for a wide range of analytical possibilities.

Analysis and Visualization - The final step is to analyze and visualize your data model. You can do this using Excel's native features like PivotTables and charts. However, because you've used Power Pivot, these will be much more dynamic and powerful than standard Pivot Tables and charts. You can easily slice and dice your data, create complex aggregations, and even build interactive dashboards.

Handling Multidimensional Data

Multidimensional data refers to data that exists in more than two dimensions. In Excel, you often work with two-dimensional data laid out in rows and columns. However, there are situations where you need to consider additional dimensions, such as time, categories, or geographical locations. Excel provides several features to handle such data, including 3D references and tables.

3D References

3D references in Excel are a tool for handling data that spans multiple worksheets. This feature allows you to refer to the same cell or range of cells across different sheets, making it incredibly useful for datasets with the same layout across multiple tabs. For instance, if you have monthly sales data for each year spread across different sheets, 3D references can simplify your calculations.

The basic syntax for a 3D reference is as follows:
=SUM(Sheet1:Sheet3!A1)

This formula will sum up the value in cell A1 across three sheets named Sheet1, Sheet2, and Sheet3.

Imagine you have an Excel workbook with 12 sheets, each representing sales data for a different month. Each sheet has the same layout. You can use a 3D reference to calculate the total annual sales without having to create a formula that references each sheet individually.

While the basic syntax is simple, 3D references can be used in more complex formulas to perform a variety of tasks. For instance, you can combine 3D references with other Excel functions like **AVERAGE**, **MIN**, and **MAX**.

Syntax Examples:

- Average: =AVERAGE(Sheet1:Sheet3!A1:A10)

- Minimum: =MIN(Sheet1:Sheet3!B1:B10)

- Maximum: =MAX(Sheet1:Sheet3!C1:C10)

Best Practices:

- Be cautious when adding or deleting sheets within the range of your 3D reference, as this can affect your calculations.

- Always double-check your 3D references if you're rearranging sheets in your workbook.

- Consider using named ranges for more clarity in your formulas.

Tables

Excel tables are another powerful feature for managing two-dimensional data. However, when combined with other features like slicers or PivotTables, they become a powerful tool for managing multidimensional data.

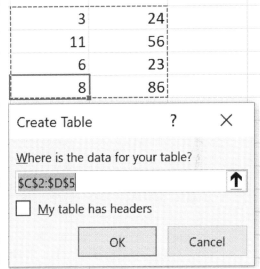

To create a table, select your data range and navigate to **Insert > Table**. This action will enable various table-specific features like auto-filtering and calculated columns.

Tables in Excel offer a range of advanced features that make handling multidimensional data easier.

Calculated Columns: You can add calculated columns to your table, which automatically fill down to include additional rows. For example, if you have a sales table with columns for 'Quantity' and 'Price,' you could add a calculated column for 'Total Sales.'

Slicers: Slicers offer a user-friendly way to filter table data, particularly when dealing with multidimensional data, making it easy to filter on multiple criteria.

Table Styles: Excel provides several built-in table styles that not only make your table visually appealing but also help in distinguishing between different types of data.

Practical Applications

Inventory Management: Use tables to keep track of product inventory across multiple locations. Add columns for each location and use slicers to view inventory levels by location.

Budgeting: Create a table to manage budgets for different departments. Use calculated columns to compute variances and slicers to filter by department.

Best Practices:

- Always give your table a descriptive name. This makes it easier to reference in formulas and makes your workbook more manageable.

- Use the 'Total Row' feature to quickly perform calculations like sum, average, or count on your table columns.

- Leverage the 'Sort and Filter' options to easily organize your multidimensional data.

The Power of Synergy

One of the most effective ways to handle complex data scenarios in Excel is by combining 3D references and tables. This approach lets you harness the best of both features, enabling you to manage and analyze multidimensional data in a more streamlined and efficient manner.

How to Combine 3D References and Tables

Imagine you have sales data for different products across multiple years, and each year's data is on a separate sheet. You can use 3D references to pull this data into a single table on a summary sheet. Once the data is in a table format, you can leverage all the advanced table features like calculated columns, slicers and even use this table as the source for a PivotTable. This gives you a powerful, centralized tool for multidimensional data analysis.

Example:

1. Use a 3D reference to sum up annual sales for a product across multiple sheets: =SUM(2020:2022!B2)

2. Place this formula in a table column named 'Total Sales.'

3. Use slicers to filter this table by product type, region, or any other relevant criteria.

4. Create a PivotTable based on this summary table to perform more advanced analyses, like finding the average annual sales growth.

Tips:

- *Descriptive Naming*: Always name your sheets and table columns descriptively. This practice not only makes it easier to create 3D references but also makes your workbook more understandable to others (or yourself at a later date).

- *Caution with Sheet Operations*: Be extra cautious when deleting or rearranging sheets that are part of a 3D reference. Such actions can break your formulas and disrupt your data analysis workflow.

- *Data Validation*: When dealing with multidimensional data that spans both multiple sheets and tables, it's crucial to maintain data integrity. Use Excel's data validation features to ensure consistency within your tables. For example, you can set up dropdown lists for categorical columns to prevent data entry errors.

Advanced Charting Techniques

Excel offers many charting options, but sometimes, the standard charts just don't cut it when you need to convey complex data insights. Advanced charting techniques can help you go beyond the basics, offering more nuanced and specialized ways to present data. If you're interested in creating interactive dashboards, multi-axis charts, or custom visualizations, advanced charting can enhance your data presentation.

Types of Advanced Charts

Waterfall charts can be used for visualizing a sequence of positive and negative values and their cumulative effect. This makes them ideal for financial analysis, such as understanding how a company arrived at its net profit starting from its gross revenue. Each column in the chart represents a financial item that either increases or decreases the final value.

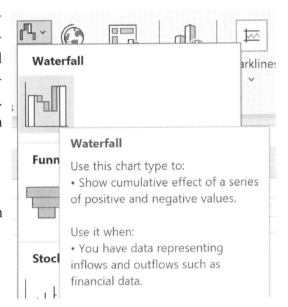

How to Create:

1. Go to the 'Insert' tab and select 'Waterfall' from the 'Charts' group.

2. Select your data range and click 'OK.'

Practical Applications:

- Cash Flow Analysis: Track the inflows and outflows over a period.

- Inventory Management: Visualize the stages of inventory from received and sold to remaining stock.

Box and Whisker Plots are excellent for statistical analysis, providing a visual representation of data distribution. The 'box' shows the quartiles of the dataset, while the 'whiskers' indicate variability outside the upper and lower quartiles. This helps you identify outliers and understand the spread and skewness of your data.

How to Create:

1. Go to the 'Insert' tab and select 'Box & Whisker' from the 'Charts' group.

2. Highlight the data you want to analyze and click 'OK.'

Practical Applications:

- Quality Control: Identify outliers in manufacturing processes.
- Exam Score Analysis: Understand the distribution of scores in a class.

Radar charts are used for displaying multivariate data on multiple axes starting from the same point. This is particularly a great feature for comparing several quantitative variables, making them ideal for performance reviews or product comparisons.

How to Create:

1. Go to the 'Insert' tab and select 'Radar' from the 'Charts' group.

2. Choose your data range and click 'OK.'

Practical Applications:

- Employee Performance: Compare various performance metrics for employees.
- Product Features: Evaluate multiple products based on several features.

Heat maps use color gradients to represent data values in a two-dimensional space, making it easier to spot trends, patterns, and outliers at a glance. The colors can represent any range of values, from low to high or vice versa.

How to Create:

1. Heat maps can be created using Excel's 'Conditional Formatting' feature. Select your data range, go to 'Home' > 'Conditional Formatting' > 'Color Scales.'

2. Choose a color scheme that fits your data.

Practical Applications:

- Sales Data: Identify high and low-performing regions.
- Website Analytics: Understand user behavior on different parts of a webpage.

Customization Techniques

One of the most effective ways to enhance the interpretability of your advanced charts is by adding custom data labels and annotations. These elements can provide immediate context to the viewer, explaining what specific data points or trends signify. For example, in a waterfall chart that shows a company's financial journey from revenue to net profit, annotations can be used to highlight significant expenses or gains.

Interactive charts offer a dynamic user experience and are particularly useful in dashboards and presentations. By incorporating form controls like sliders, checkboxes, or drop-down menus, you allow the audience to manipulate the data view in real-time. This interactivity can be especially beneficial for exploring large or complex datasets, as it enables users to focus on specific aspects without feeling overwhelmed.

In a fast-paced environment where data is continually being updated, having to manually adjust your charts can be a significant drawback. This is where dynamic ranges come into play. By defining named ranges and using Excel functions like **OFFSET** and **COUNTA**, you can set your charts to update automatically when new data is added to the dataset. This ensures that your charts always represent the most current information without requiring constant manual intervention.

Best Practices

Consistency in Design - One of the best practices in advanced charting is maintaining a consistent design language. This includes using a uniform color scheme, font, and layout across all charts within a report or presentation. Consistency helps in creating a cohesive and professional look, making it easier for the audience to focus on the data rather than getting distracted by varying styles.

The Art of Simplicity - Advanced charts come with various customization options, but it's crucial to remember that simplicity often trumps complexity. The main objective is to facilitate understanding. Avoid adding too many data series, labels, or decorative elements that could clutter the chart and confuse the viewer.

Data Integrity and Verification - Before you even start charting, ensure that the data you're using is accurate and up-to-date. Verify your data sources and double-check any formulas you've used for calculations. A visually stunning chart loses all its value if the underlying data is flawed or outdated.

User-Centric Testing - Once you've created an advanced chart, it's advisable to test its effectiveness by showing it to a sample of your target audience. This can offer valuable insights into the chart's effectiveness in conveying the intended information and whether any elements are causing confusion or potential misinterpretation. Based on the feedback, you can make the necessary adjustments.

Chapter Seven

DAY 7: MASTERING EXCEL

As we reach the end of our week-long journey through Excel's extensive features, today's focus shifts toward mastery. This final chapter is designed to polish your skills, streamline your tasks, and ensure that you're making the most of everything Excel has to offer.

We'll kick things off by focusing on workflow optimization, teaching you how to perform tasks more efficiently through shortcuts and custom functions. Then, we'll explore how Excel doesn't exist in a vacuum by talking about its integration with other Office applications.

Security is paramount in any data-related work, so we'll discover how to safeguard your worksheets and workbooks. I'll also aim to keep you ahead of the curve by discussing how to stay updated with Excel's ever-evolving features and capabilities.

Finally, because practice makes perfect, I'll offer guidance on how to further refine your Excel skills through a structured study routine and additional resources.

So, let's get started on this final leg of your Excel mastery journey!

Optimizing Workflow

The more efficiently you can navigate and manipulate data, the more time you can allocate to analysis and decision-making. This is where shortcuts and custom functions step into the spotlight.

Shortcuts: Your Best Friend in Excel

Keyboard shortcuts are more than just a way to save a few seconds here and there. They are a fundamental component of an efficient workflow in Excel. The cumulative time saved by using shortcuts can be substantial, freeing you up to focus on more complex tasks that require critical thinking.

Shortcuts in Excel can be broadly categorized into several types based on their functionality:

Navigation Shortcuts help you move around your worksheet effortlessly.

- Ctrl + Arrow Key: Move to the edge of data region
- Alt + Page Down: Move one screen to the right

Data Manipulation Shortcuts are used for editing and arranging data.

- Ctrl + D: Fill down
- Ctrl + R: Fill right

Formatting Shortcuts help you quickly format your cells.

- Ctrl + 1: Open the Format Cells dialog box
- Alt + H, V, F: Paste only formulas

Calculation Shortcuts are used for quick calculations.

- F9: Calculate all worksheets
- Shift + F9: Calculate active worksheet

Advanced Shortcuts – For users who are comfortable with the basics, there are advanced shortcuts that can perform complex tasks:

- Alt + E, S, T: Paste formats
- Ctrl + Alt + V, M: Paste values and number formats

Creating Your Own Shortcuts

While Excel provides numerous built-in shortcuts, there might be instances where you require a shortcut for a specific task that lacks one. In such cases, you can create your own shortcuts using Excel's Quick Access Toolbar or even by writing a small macro in VBA.

Tips for Mastering Shortcuts

Practice: The more you use shortcuts, the more intuitive they become.

Cheat Sheet: Create a cheat sheet of your most-used shortcuts and keep it handy.

Shortcut of the Day: Each day, pick a new shortcut to learn and use it throughout the day.

Custom Functions: Tailoring Excel to Your Needs

Excel boasts an extensive selection of ready-to-use functions, covering everything from simple arithmetic operations to advanced statistical analyses. However, there are instances where these built-in options fall short of your specific needs. Custom functions allow you to define your own calculations, giving you the flexibility to perform tasks that are unique to your work or industry.

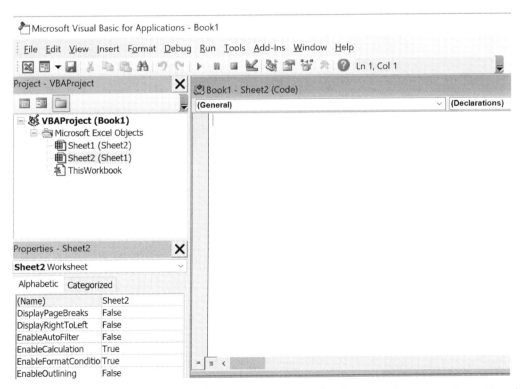

Creating a custom function involves a few steps but can be incredibly rewarding. Here's how to go about it:

    1. *Open the VBA Editor*: Press **Alt + F11** to open the Visual Basic for Applications (VBA) editor.

2. *Insert a New Module:* In the VBA editor, right-click on any existing module in the Project Explorer and choose **Insert > Module.**

3. *Write the Function:* In the new module window, you can start writing your custom function using VBA syntax. Make sure to define the function with a Function statement and end it with an **End Function** statement.

4. *Debug and Test:* Before saving, run some tests to ensure the function works as expected. Debug if necessary.

5. *Save and Close:* Once you're satisfied with your custom function, save the module and close the VBA editor.

Keyboard and Mouse Tricks

Excel is not just about formulas and functions; it's also about how efficiently you can navigate and manipulate data. Mastering lesser-known mouse operations can significantly enhance your productivity and streamline your workflow.

Lesser-Known Mouse Operations

Mouse operations in Excel are often underutilized. While most users are familiar with basic clicking and dragging, Excel offers a range of advanced mouse operations that can make your work much more efficient.

Examples and Uses:

1. Ctrl + Drag for Copying Cells

Holding down the Ctrl key while dragging a cell will copy the cell's content to the new location. This is a lifesaver when you want to duplicate data across multiple cells without having to copy and paste.

Pro Tip: You can also use Ctrl + Drag to copy entire rows or columns.

2. Right-Click Drag for Multiple Options

When you drag cells with the right mouse button, a context menu appears, giving you options to copy, move, or even insert copied cells. You can count on these options when you're unsure whether to copy or move data and want to decide on the fly.

Pro Tip: Use this feature to quickly create drop-down menus for cells.

3. Double-Click Fill Handle for Auto-Fill

Double-clicking the fill handle (the small square at the bottom-right corner of a selected cell) will auto-fill cells down the column until it reaches the end of the adjacent data. This is a time-saver when you have a long column of data that you want to fill based on a pattern or formula.

Pro Tip: You can also drag the fill handle horizontally to auto-fill rows.

4. *Shift + Scroll Wheel for Horizontal Scrolling*

Using the scroll wheel while holding down the Shift key allows you to scroll horizontally. When working with wide spreadsheets where you need to move from one end to the other frequently, this can be quite useful.

Pro Tip: Combine this with Ctrl + Scroll Wheel to zoom in and out, making navigation even more efficient.

Customizing the Quick Access Toolbar

The Quick Access Toolbar (QAT) is a customizable toolbar located at the top of the Excel window. It allows you to add shortcuts to various commands and features, making your mouse more efficient by reducing the number of clicks needed to perform an action.

How to Customize Basic Features

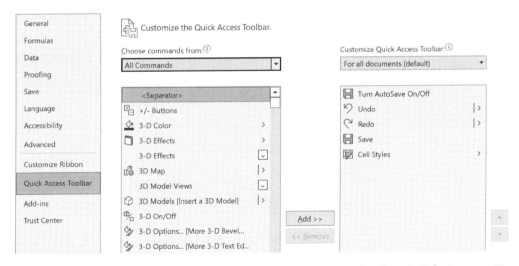

1. *Right-Click on Toolbar*: Right-click on an empty space in the Quick Access Toolbar and select 'Customize Quick Access Toolbar.'

2. *Choose Commands*: A dialog box will appear with a list of all available Excel commands. Select the ones you use most frequently and click 'Add.'

3. *Organize*: You can rearrange the order of the commands by selecting them and using the 'Move Up' and 'Move Down' buttons.

4. *Save*: Once you've completed your customization and are satisfied with your adjustments, click 'OK' to save your changes.

Advanced Customization Techniques

Import and Export Customizations: It allows you to share your customized QAT with others or apply it to other computers you use.

How to Do It: Go to the 'Customize Quick Access Toolbar' dialog box, click on 'Import/Export' at the bottom, and choose 'Export all customizations' to save your current setup as a file or 'Import customization file' to load a previously saved setup.

Add Macros to the Quick Access Toolbar: Enables quick access to frequently used macros.

How to Do It: Right-click on the toolbar, select 'Customize Quick Access Toolbar,' choose 'Macros' from the 'Choose commands from' dropdown, and click 'Add.'

Add Separator Lines for Better Organization: Adds a visual separator between groups of related commands.

How to Do It: Open the 'Customize Quick Access Toolbar' dialog box, select '<Separator>' from the 'Choose commands from' dropdown, and click 'Add.'

Keyboard Shortcuts for Quick Access Toolbar: It allows you to use the keyboard to quickly select commands from the QAT.

How to Do It: Press the 'Alt' key, and Excel will display a number for each command on the QAT. Press the corresponding number to activate that command.

Integration with Other Office Applications

Microsoft Office is a suite of applications designed to work seamlessly together, and Excel is no exception. Integrating Excel with other Office tools, such as Word, PowerPoint, and Outlook, can optimize your workflow, minimize manual data entry, and boost the overall efficiency of your tasks.

Excel and Word: Dynamic Data Embedding

One of the most common integrations is between Excel and Word. You can embed Excel tables, charts, or even entire spreadsheets into a Word document, which is pretty useful for creating dynamic reports where the data may change over time. Any updates made to the Excel file can be automatically reflected in the Word document, ensuring that you're always presenting the most current data.

Excel and PowerPoint: Data Visualization

PowerPoint is another application where Excel integration comes in handy. You can embed Excel charts into your PowerPoint slides for more dynamic and data-driven presentations. Just like with Word, any changes to the original Excel chart can be updated in PowerPoint with just a few clicks.

Excel and Outlook: Automating Tasks

Excel can also integrate with Outlook to automate various tasks. For example, you can set up a macro in Excel that sends an email through Outlook whenever a certain condition is met in your spreadsheet, such as reaching a sales target or inventory threshold.

Excel and Access: Data Management

For more complex data management tasks, Excel can be integrated with Microsoft Access. You can import data from an Access database into Excel for analysis or export Excel data into Access for more strong data management and querying capabilities.

How to Integrate

The basic steps for integrating Excel with other Office applications are quite easy, but it's the nuances that can make your integration more effective. Let's find out how we can do it:

1. Locate the 'Insert' Tab: Open the Office application you wish to integrate with Excel, such as Word or PowerPoint. Navigate to the 'Insert' tab on the ribbon at the top.

2. Choose Object: Within the 'Insert' tab, locate and click on the 'Object' button. A dialog box will appear, presenting you with various object types to insert. Select 'Microsoft Excel Worksheet' for embedding a spreadsheet or 'Microsoft Excel Chart' for a chart.

3. Embed or Link:

- Embedding: This option inserts a copy of the Excel object directly into your document. It becomes part of the document and is independent of the original Excel file.

- Linking: This creates a dynamic link to the Excel file. Any changes made to the original Excel file will be reflected in the document where it's linked. You'll usually see an option like 'Link to file' in the dialog box.

4. Update as Needed:

- For Embedded Objects: Since the object is a static copy, you'll need to manually update it if the original Excel file changes.

- For Linked Objects: You can right-click on the object and select 'Update Link' to refresh the data.

Best Practices

- *File Paths*: When linking Excel files, ensure that the linked files are stored in a location accessible to anyone using the integrated document. Network drives or shared cloud storage are often good options.

- *Version Compatibility*: Different versions of Office applications may not play well together. To avoid any compatibility issues, make sure all your Office applications are updated to the same version.

- *Data Security / Embedding*: Remember that embedded objects become part of the document. If the document is shared, the embedded data is shared as well.

- *Data Security / Linking*: Linked data remains in the original Excel file. However, anyone with access to the integrated document could potentially access the linked Excel file as well. Always be cautious with sensitive data.

- *Performance*: Linking to large Excel files can slow down the performance of your Word document or PowerPoint presentation. Be mindful of file sizes and consider whether embedding might be a more efficient option in such cases.

- *Error Handling*: Especially for linked objects, ensure you have robust error-handling procedures. Broken links can result in errors or missing data in your integrated document.

Excel Security

Excel is often the go-to tool for businesses and individuals alike for data storage and analysis. Given the sensitive nature of the data it often holds, implementing robust security measures is not just advisable but essential. The objective is to safeguard against unauthorized access, accidental deletions, and unauthorized modifications, thereby guaranteeing both data integrity and confidentiality.

Detailed Types of Protection

Worksheet Protection:

- Cell Locking: By default, all cells in a worksheet are locked. However, this doesn't take effect until you enable worksheet protection. This is useful for safeguarding key formulas or confidential data.

- Feature Restrictions: You can disable specific functionalities like the ability to insert images, hyperlinks, or even new worksheets.

- Range Permissions: Excel allows you to set permissions for different ranges within a single worksheet, enabling multiple users to work on a sheet while restricting their access to specific cells.

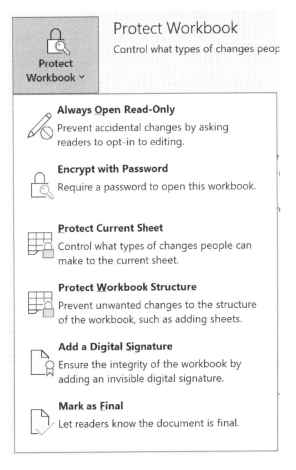

Workbook Protection:

- Structure Protection: This prevents users from changing the workbook's overall structure, such as adding new worksheets or deleting existing ones.

- Window Protection: This locks the size and position of the workbook's window, preventing users from moving, resizing, or closing it.

- Revision Tracking: When this feature is enabled, Excel keeps track of the changes made, allowing you to review them later.

File Encryption:

- Password Protection: This is the simplest form of Excel security. A password is required to open the file, providing a first line of defense against unauthorized access.

- Certificate Encryption: For even stronger security, you can use certificate encryption. This requires a digital certificate to open the file.

Implementing Security Measures: A Step-by-Step Guide

Worksheet Protection:

1. Go to the 'Review' tab.

2. Click on 'Protect Sheet.'

3. Choose the functionalities you want to allow or restrict and set a password.

Workbook Protection:

1. Navigate to the 'Review' tab.

2. Select 'Protect Workbook.'

3. Choose between protecting the structure and/or the windows and set a password.

File Encryption:

1. Click on the 'File' tab.

2. Go to 'Info.'

3. Under 'Protect Workbook,' choose 'Encrypt with Password' and set your password.

Advanced Security Tips

The Importance of Strong Passwords - One of the most fundamental yet often overlooked aspects of Excel security is the use of strong, unique passwords. A strong password typically includes a mix of upper and lower-case letters, numbers, and special characters. The longer and more complex the password, the more secure your Excel files will be. Avoid using easily guessable information like birthdays, names, or common words.

Keeping Software Up to Date - Software vulnerabilities are a common entry point for unauthorized access. Microsoft regularly releases security patches and updates for Excel to address these vulnerabilities. Make it a habit to update your software as soon as these patches are released. This not only enhances security but also provides you with new features and performance improvements.

User Education and Training - Human error is often the weakest link in any security chain. Training users about the importance of Excel security can go a long way in preventing breaches. Educate them on the following:

- The risks of sharing passwords.

- How to identify phishing emails or malicious software that may compromise Excel files.

- The importance of logging out of shared computers to prevent unauthorized access.

The Necessity of Backups - Data loss can happen in many ways, from accidental deletion to file corruption. Having a secure and up-to-date backup ensures that you can quickly recover your data when needed. Use automated backup solutions that store data in a secure, offsite location. Also, consider encrypting your backup for an added layer of security.

Implementing Audit Trails - For Excel files containing highly sensitive or regulated data, auditing is crucial. Excel's built-in auditing features allow you to track changes made to the workbook. For more advanced needs, there are third-party tools that provide detailed audit trails, showing who accessed the file, what changes were made, and when. This is useful for compliance with data protection regulations and for internal investigations.

Staying Ahead with Excel

Keeping your Excel software up-to-date is not just about security; it's also about taking advantage of new features and improvements that can enhance your productivity. Microsoft frequently releases updates that include new functionalities, bug fixes, and performance enhancements. Ignoring these updates means you're missing out on tools that could make your work easier and more efficient.

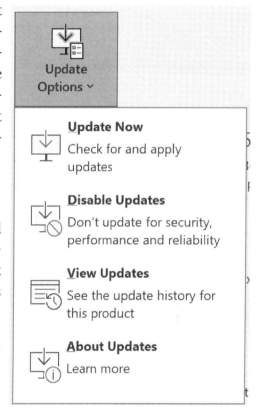

How to Update Excel

Automatic Updates: If you're using a subscription-based version of Excel, updates are usually downloaded and installed automatically. However, you can manually check for updates by going to **File > Account > Update Options > Update Now.**

Manual Updates: For standalone versions, you'll need to download and install updates manually. Visit the Microsoft Update Catalog website to find the latest patches.

Whenever an update is released, take some time to explore what's new. Microsoft provides detailed release notes that outline new features, improvements, and fixes. Some updates may introduce features that are highly relevant to your work, such as new chart types, advanced formulas, or enhanced data analysis tools.

If you're keen on getting early access to new features, consider joining the Office Insider program. This allows you to test new features before they are released to the general public. However, be cautious when using Insider builds for critical tasks, as they may contain bugs.

Following Official Channels and Communities

Stay informed by following Microsoft's official blogs, forums, and social media channels. These platforms offer valuable tips, tutorials, and announcements about upcoming features. Participating in Excel-related online communities can also provide valuable information on how others are utilizing new features and the challenges they might be facing.

Excel for Mobile Devices

The advent of smartphones and tablets has revolutionized the way we interact with software applications, and Microsoft Excel is no exception. Excel's mobile app offers a convenient way to work on spreadsheets on the go, but it's important to understand how it differs from the desktop version and how to use it effectively.

How Excel's Mobile App Differs from the Desktop Version

1. Limited Features: The mobile app doesn't have all the functionalities of the desktop version. For example, features like Power Query, VBA macros, and some advanced chart types are not available on mobile.

2. User Interface: The mobile app is designed for touch, making the interface more streamlined. Menus and options are simplified to fit the smaller screen and touch navigation.

3. File Access: On mobile, you can easily access files stored in cloud services like OneDrive or Dropbox, making it easier to work on the go.

4. Collaboration: The mobile app is designed with quick, real-time collaboration in mind. You can easily share files and collaborate with others directly from the app.

5. Offline Access: While the desktop version is generally used in an always-on environment, the mobile app allows for offline editing, which can then be synced when you're back online.

6. AutoSave: The mobile app often has AutoSave enabled by default, which automatically saves changes as you make them.

Tips for Using Excel Effectively on Mobile Devices

1. Start Simple: Due to the limited screen size and functionalities, it's best to start with simple spreadsheets. Complex models with lots of data might be complicated to manage on a mobile device.

2. Use Templates: The mobile app offers various templates for everyday tasks like budgeting, scheduling, and invoicing. Utilize these to quickly create spreadsheets.

3. Zoom and Navigate: Use pinch-to-zoom to focus on specific cells or areas of your spreadsheet. Also, familiarize yourself with navigation shortcuts specific to your device.

4. Voice Commands: Many mobile devices allow for voice input, which can be a quick way to enter data or execute commands.

5. External Keyboards: If you have a lot of data entry or complex calculations, consider using an external Bluetooth keyboard for better efficiency.

6. Cloud Sync: Always ensure that your work is being synced to the cloud. This not only serves as a backup but also allows you to seamlessly switch between devices.

7. Review and Edit: While the mobile app is great for quick edits and reviews, for more complex tasks, it's often better to switch to the desktop version. Make sure to review your work on a larger screen to catch any errors or formatting issues.

8. Battery Life: Keep an eye on your device's battery life, especially if you're working on large spreadsheets or for an extended period.

9. Data Security: Just like on a desktop, ensure that any sensitive data is adequately protected, especially if you're using a shared or public network.

Excel Troubleshooting

Even the most seasoned Excel users can encounter errors or issues that disrupt their workflow. Knowing how to troubleshoot these problems effectively can save you time and frustration. Below are some common errors and issues you might come across while using Excel, along with strategies for resolving them.

Common Errors and Issues

#VALUE! Error

The #VALUE! error is Excel's way of saying that a formula is expecting a certain type of value but receives another. For instance, if you try to subtract a text string from a number, Excel will display this error.

Common Scenarios:

- Subtracting a text value from a number: **=A1 - "text"**
- Using a function that expects a number but receives text: **=SQRT("text")**

How to Fix:

1. *Check Cell Data Types*: Make sure that the cells referenced in your formula contain the correct data types.

2. *Use Excel's Type Functions*: Functions like **ISNUMBER()** or **ISTEXT()** can help you identify the type of data you're dealing with.

3. *Error-Handling Functions*: Use functions like **IFERROR()** to handle possible errors grace-

fully.

#REF! Error

The #REF! error occurs when a formula refers to a cell that is no longer available, often because it has been deleted or moved.

Common Scenarios:

- Deleting a row or column that is being referenced by a formula.
- Cutting a cell and pasting it in a location that disrupts a formula.

How to Fix:

1. *Undo the Action*: If you've just deleted a row or column, undoing the action (Ctrl + Z) can often fix the error.
2. *Update References*: Manually adjust the formula to refer to the correct cells.
3. *Use Structured References*: If you're working with tables, structured references can prevent this error.

#NAME? Error

The #NAME? Error is displayed when Excel doesn't recognize text within a formula. This often happens when function names are misspelled or when quotation marks are missing around text values.

Common Scenarios:

- Misspelling a function name: **=SUMM(A1:A10)**
- Forgetting quotation marks around text: **=VLOOKUP(A1, A2:A10, 2, Flase)**

How to Fix:

1. *Check Spelling*: Ensure that all function names are spelled correctly.
2. *Verify Quotation Marks*: Make sure that text values are enclosed in quotation marks.
3. *Check for Extra Spaces*: Extra spaces before or after function names can also trigger this error.

#DIV/0! Error

The #DIV/0! error occurs when a number is divided by zero, which is mathematically undefined.

Common Scenarios:

- Dividing a number by zero: **=A1/0**

- Dividing a number by a cell that contains zero: **=A1/B1** where B1 contains zero.

How to Fix:

1. *Check the Denominator*: Make sure the cell or value you're dividing by is not zero.

2. *Use Conditional Formulas*: Utilize **IF()** or **IFERROR()** to handle zero values in the denominator. For example, **=IF(B1=0, "Cannot divide by zero", A1/B1)**

File Corruption

File corruption refers to a situation where an Excel file becomes damaged or altered in such a way that it cannot be opened or function properly.

Common Scenarios:

- Abrupt system shutdown while the Excel file is open.

- Virus or malware infection.

- Disk errors or bad sectors on the storage medium.

How to Fix:

1. Use Open and Repair: Excel has a built-in 'Open and Repair' feature that can sometimes fix corrupted files.

2. Restore from Backup: If you have a backup of the file, restoring it is often the quickest solution.

3. Third-Party Tools: Various software tools are available that claim to repair corrupted Excel files, although their effectiveness can vary.

Slow Performance

Slow performance in Excel can occur for a variety of reasons but is most commonly due to large file sizes or complex calculations that require a lot of processing power.

Common Scenarios:

- Files with thousands of rows and columns.

- Complex formulas or extensive use of volatile functions like **INDIRECT()**.

- Multiple pivot tables, charts, or embedded objects.

How to Fix:

1. Optimize Formulas: Use more efficient formulas and functions where possible.

2. Limit Use of Volatile Functions: Functions like **INDIRECT()** and **OFFSET()** can slow down Excel because they cause the entire worksheet to recalculate.

3. Use Data Tables Wisely: Large data tables can slow down performance; consider using database software for very large datasets.

Macro Issues

Macro problems can crop up due to various factors, such as VBA code errors, security configurations, or clashes with other software.

Common scenarios could be:

- Macros are disabled due to security settings.
- Errors or bugs in the VBA code.
- Conflicts with other add-ins or software.

How to Fix:

1. Check Security Settings: Make sure that your security settings allow macros to run.

2. Debug the Code: Use the VBA editor's debugging tools to identify and fix errors in the code.

3. Check for Conflicts: Disable other add-ins or software that might be conflicting with the macro.

Formatting Issues

Formatting issues in Excel can range from simple annoyances, like cells that won't take on the desired format, to more complex problems, like conditional formatting rules that don't work as expected.

Common Scenarios:

- Conditional formatting rules that don't apply correctly.
- Text alignment or font issues.
- Number or date formats that don't display as expected.

How to Fix:

1. *Check Conditional Formatting Rules*: Ensure your rules are set up correctly and in the right order.

2. *Clear and Reapply Formatting*: Sometimes, clearing all formatting and starting fresh can resolve issues.

3. *Use Format Painter*: The Format Painter tool can help you quickly apply a desired format to multiple cells.

Advanced Troubleshooting and Tips

A **circular reference** occurs when a formula refers to its own cell either directly or indirectly, creating an infinite loop that can cause Excel to freeze or give incorrect results.

Circular references can lead to incorrect calculations and may cause Excel to use excessive CPU resources, slowing down your computer.

How to Resolve:

1. Identify the Circular Reference: Excel usually displays a warning about circular references. Take note of the cell that is causing the issue.

2. Break the Loop: Modify the formula so that it no longer refers to its own cell.

3. Use Iterative Calculation: If the circular reference is intentional (for some advanced calculations), you can enable iterative calculations under Excel Options > Formulas.

Data Import Issues - Common Problems:

- Missing or incomplete data
- Incorrect data types
- Encoding issues when importing text files

How to Resolve:

1. Check Source File: Ensure the source file is not corrupted and is in a compatible format.

2. Specify Data Types: When importing, specify the correct data types for each column if possible.

3. Use Data Import Wizard: Excel's Data Import Wizard offers options to handle various issues during the import process.

Formula auditing allows you to trace the relationships between cells to debug complex formulas.

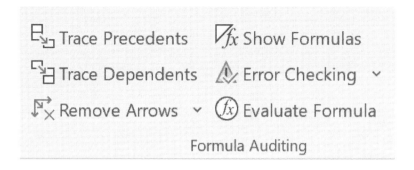

How to Use:

1. Trace Precedents/Dependents: Use these features to see which cells affect the value of the currently selected cell.

2. Error Checking: This feature will highlight cells that have errors, helping you identify issues quickly.

3. Evaluate Formula: This breaks down a formula into its components, showing the result of each part.

What to do when **Excel Crashes**:

1. Restart Excel: Often, simply restarting the application can resolve the issue.

2. Check for Updates: Make sure your Excel application is up-to-date to minimize bugs.

How to Recover Unsaved Files:

1. AutoRecover: Excel automatically saves a version of unsaved files. Go to File > Open > Recover Unsaved Workbooks.

2. Manual Recovery: If you had manually saved a version of the file, navigate to the location where it was saved and look for backup files.

Excel's "Not Responding" Issue - This issue can occur for various reasons, such as large file sizes, complex calculations, or conflicts with other software or add-ins.

How to Resolve:

1. Wait: Sometimes, Excel may be processing a large task. Give it a few moments to see if it recovers.

2. Task Manager: Use the Task Manager to end the Excel process if it's unresponsive for an extended period. Note that you may lose unsaved work.

3. Safe Mode: Open Excel in Safe Mode to see if the issue persists, which can help you determine if the problem is due to add-ins or other external factors.

Hyperlink Issues - Common Problems:

- Hyperlinks leading to the wrong location
- Hyperlinks not opening

How to Resolve:

1. Check URL: Ensure the hyperlink is correctly formatted and leads to the intended location.

2. Security Settings: Some security settings may block hyperlinks. Check your settings to ensure they allow hyperlinks to open.

3. Repair Office: Sometimes, repairing your Office installation can resolve hyperlink issues.

Keyboard Shortcuts Not Working - Common Reasons:

- Conflicts with system shortcuts
- Excel is in a mode where shortcuts are disabled (e.g., cell editing mode)

How to Fix:

1. Check Excel Mode: Ensure Excel is not in a mode that disables shortcuts.

2. Check System Shortcuts: Make sure there are no system-level shortcuts that conflict with Excel's shortcuts.

3. Reset Shortcuts: You can reset Excel's shortcuts to their default settings through the options menu.

Print Issues - Common Problems:

- Incorrect print area
- Gridlines not showing
- Text cut off

How to Resolve:

1. Set Print Area: Define the correct print area before printing.

2. Gridline Settings: Check the 'Page Layout' tab to ensure gridlines are set to print.

3. Page Setup: Use the 'Page Setup' dialog box to adjust settings like orientation, margins, and scaling.

Password Recovery - If you forget the password to an Excel sheet, you may be locked out of viewing or editing that sheet.

How to Recover:

1. Password Hint: If you've set a password hint, use it to jog your memory.

2. Contact Admin: If the sheet is part of a company workbook, the admin may be able to reset the password.

3. Third-Party Software: There are specialized software tools designed to recover Excel passwords, although their effectiveness can vary.

CONCLUSION

We have come to the end of our comprehensive 7-day journey exploring the vast capabilities of Microsoft Excel. Throughout this guide, I have provided a condensed crash course to help you get started. However, it's important to remember that learning Excel is a flexible process. You can set your own pace based on your current skills, evolving needs, and personal preferences.

Over the past week, you have learned the skills to transform this complex software into a more approachable and empowering tool. We began by familiarizing ourselves with the basics—the interface, basic operations, data entry, and formatting. Building on that foundation, we delved into formulas, functions, and logical operators, exploring the mathematical heart of Excel. We then honed our skills further by learning techniques for sorting, filtering, and visualizing real-world data sets.

As our journey progressed, we explored more advanced functionalities such as PivotTables, VLOOKUP, and macros. Along the way, I offered guidance on best practices, including workflow optimization and accessibility. By now, Excel should feel less overwhelming and more like a toolkit filled with instruments waiting to be used.

However, our learning doesn't end here. Mastery requires consistent practice and application. The best way to become proficient in Excel is to apply what you've learned to real-life scenarios in your personal, academic, or professional life. Start small—use Excel to plan a budget, organize your music library, or track your fitness progress. As your skills grow, take on more challenging projects that allow you to fully utilize the power of this software.

Remember to revisit previous chapters or seek external resources for a refresher whenever needed. Excel's capabilities are extensive, and occasional guidance will likely be helpful, no matter your skill level. Always view Excel proficiency as an ongoing pursuit instead of a fixed destination.

Above all, keep in mind that Excel is a tool that empowers people, reveals insights, and helps accomplish goals. As you improve your Excel skills, remember to stay focused on the human purposes and problems that this software can address. Let Excel enhance your capabilities while you put your skills to use in making a positive impact in the world.

The journey towards Excel excellence never truly ends because there is always more potential to discover. However, armed with the knowledge from this guide, you now have a valuable roadmap and a strong skill set to guide you wherever you decide to go.

Bring your data to life, turn insights into action, and begin your own path to Excel mastery!

Acknowledgements

First and foremost, I extend my deepest appreciation to each one of you who has chosen to accompany me on this enlightening journey through the world of Excel. Your commitment to learning and your willingness to invest in this book have been the cornerstone of my efforts.

To my family and closest friends, your unwavering support and faith in me have been my north star. Your patience and encouragement during the countless hours I spent researching, teaching, and writing have been indispensable.

A heartfelt acknowledgment to my editor and the entire publishing team. Your expertise, constructive criticism, and relentless commitment have molded "Excel 2024: From Beginner to Advanced in 7 Days" into the comprehensive resource it is today.

To you, esteemed reader, thank you for dedicating your time and energy to explore the multifaceted world of Excel through these pages. Whether you're an absolute beginner, a hobbyist, or an aspiring professional, I hope this book serves as a valuable guide, steering you toward a more adept and confident understanding of Excel.

If this book has struck a chord with you, I kindly request a small favor. Please consider leaving a review on Amazon. Your insights are not only crucial for my development as an author but also for aiding potential readers in recognizing the practical advantages of mastering Excel.

With sincere gratitude,

Derek Collins

EXCLUSIVE BONUS: ACCESS YOUR EXCEL RESOURCE KIT!

Dear valued reader,

To elevate the learning experience initiated with our Excel manual, we are pleased to offer you a collection of exclusive bonus resources. These additional tools are curated to enhance your proficiency in Excel, ensuring a more thorough and effective educational experience.

1. 500 Key Excel Formulas Cheat Sheet
2. 130+ Ready-to-Use Excel Templates
3. Excel 2024: The PDF Portable Edition
4. Audiobook "The Art of Decision Making"
5. Practical Video Tutorials

Scan the QR code below to access all the bonus materials!

BEST ONLINE RESOURCES

Scan the QR codes below to access all the resources

 Excel ChatGPT Tutor for Beginners

 Practice Excel Online for Free

 MS Excel Video Training

 Excel Exercises

 Chandoo.org Become Awesome in Excel

 Excel Skills for Business (Coursera)

 Excel Easy Tutorials

 Reddit Excel Community r/excel

Made in United States
Troutdale, OR
03/03/2024